D0563900

THE ESSENTIAL POETS

THE ESSENTIAL
BYRON

George Gordon, the sixth Lord Byron

BORN   22 JANUARY 1788
DIED   19 APRIL 1824

THE ESSENTIAL
BYRON

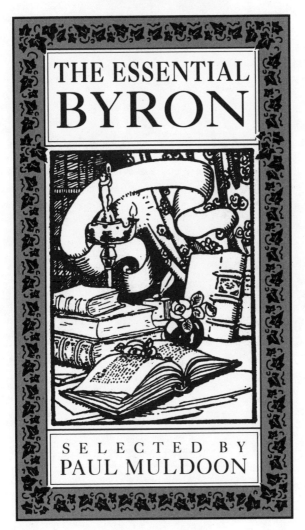

SELECTED BY
PAUL MULDOON

GALAHAD BOOKS
NEW YORK

Published in 1992 by

Galahad Books
A division of LDAP, Inc.
386 Park Avenue South
New York, New York 10016

Galahad Books is a registered trademark of LDAP, Inc.

This edition published by arrangement with The Ecco Press.

ISBN: 0-88365-803-8

Original design by Reg Perry
Additional art and design for this edition by Cindy LaBreacht

Portrait of Lord Byron
by Thomas Phillips,
Courtesy of Newstead Abbey,
Nottingham Museums.

Printed in the United States of America

CONTENTS

THE ESSENTIAL
BYRON

❧ INTRODUCTION ❧

I want to begin with a dictionary definition of the term *Byronic: "adj.* possessing the characteristics of Lord Byron, or of his poetry, over-strained in sentiment or passion, cynical and libertine." That the name of a poet who is now comparatively little-read should have entered the language on account of his life rather than his work is an irony that he himself would have savored, however bitterly. Byron once wrote to his friend, the Irish "melodist" Tom Moore, who had recently been the subject of a biography: "The biographer has made a botch of your life. . . . If that damned fellow was to write *my* life, I would certainly take *his.*" As it turned out, Moore would himself write a *Life of Byron,* and in a review of that book Macaulay would give a thumbnail sketch of the so-called Byronic hero, "a man proud, moody, cynical, with defiance on his brow and misery in his heart, a scorner of his kind, implacable in revenge, yet capable of deep and strong affection." It is the confusion in the popular imagination between the Byronic hero and Byron himself that has dogged generations of his readers.

That confusion does not seem to be *entirely* unfounded when one considers the facts of his life. His great modern biographer, Leslie Marchand, begins: "George Gordon, the sixth Lord Byron, was born with a lame right foot on January 22nd, 1788." This handicap, which modern surgery could almost certainly have minimized, may account for Byron's inclination to compensate with feats of physical stamina and derring-do, such as his famous swimming of the Hellespont. His mother's mood fluctuated from cosseting to contemptuous—she once referred to him as "a lame brat"—while his father, a dissolute Scots Peer, was uniformly dislikable; he finally ran out on the family when

| 3 |

George was two years old. At the age of ten the boy succeeded to the title on the death of an uncle, and the new Lord Byron left London for the family seat at Newstead Abbey, near Nottingham.

In due course, Byron went to school at Harrow and then to the university of Cambridge, where he began to write the poems that were eventually published under the title *Hours of Idleness* (1807), a dismissive notice of which appeared in *The Edinburgh Review*. This prompted Byron's first major work, *English Bards and Scotch Reviewers* (1809), an exuberant, excoriating attack on the fashionable critics and poets of the day, including Wordsworth, Coleridge, and, above all, Robert Southey, his favorite *bête noire*. The extracts I've included here give some clue not only to Byron's enemies but also his heroes, preeminent among whom is Alexander Pope; already Byron had taken Pope's couplet and made it his own, investing it with the languorous cutting edge that would typify his later long poems.

In 1809 Byron also made his first trip to the Mediterranean and began *Childe Harold's Pilgrimage,* which was published in 1812 to great popular acclaim; as Byron put it, "I awoke one morning and found myself famous." He was particularly flattered by his reception in the New World: "These are the first tidings that ever sounded like Fame to my ears—to be redde [*sic*] on the banks of the Ohio!" *Childe Harold* was followed by a series of poems, *The Giaour, The Bride of Abydos, The Corsair,* and *Lara,* that gratified the public demand for romantic adventure stories. Byron's own romantic adventures were also the subject of public scrutiny: there was the affair with a married woman, Lady Caroline Lamb, who characterized him as "mad, bad and dangerous to know"; there was the incestuous affair with his half-sister, Augusta Leigh; there was the short-lived marriage to Annabella Millbanks. In the midst of rumor and speculation, Byron left England in 1816, never to return. On his last night in Dover, he visited the grave of the eighteenth-century satiric poet Charles Churchill, for whom he had

some fellow feeling; like Churchill, Byron had been the flavor of the month, "the comet of a season."

For the next seven years, Byron lived mostly in Italy, where he gave himself over to "sleep, eating and swilling, buttoning and unbuttoning" and the writing of poems—the further peregrinations of *Childe Harold, The Prisoner of Chillon, Manfred, Mazeppa,* and my own favorite, *Beppo,* which I've included in its entirety. In *Beppo* (1818) we see Byron at his brilliant best—witty, wise, at one moment stepping on the gas and cruising along the narrative equivalent of a six-lane highway, at the next content to pull over and make a leisurely digression down some back road or blind alley.

I must myself digress to explain something of my thinking in making this present selection. If you're already familiar with Byron's work you will, I hope, understand my dilemma; stated bluntly, it is that while this volume is necessarily short, the best of Byron's poems are often very long. I wanted to avoid as much as possible the chopping up of poems into kindling, but could not (as with *Don Juan*) manage it entirely. On the other hand, my choice of a complete, longer poem like *Beppo* over, say, *The Siege of Corinth* may strike some readers as being merely whimsical. That, I'm afraid, is a risk I have to take. Another longer piece I chose to reprint in full is *The Vision of Judgement* (1822), which was prompted by a poem of the same title by Southey, who had become Poet Laureate and exchanged his erstwhile radical republicanism for unabashed royalism. Here the slow burn of Byron's invective makes his occasional pieces on another political enemy, Robert Stewart, Viscount Castlereagh and second Marquis of Londonderry, look like damp squibs by comparison. For the ultimate fireworks display one turns, of course, to *Don Juan,* all five hundred seemingly effortless pages of it. Byron's mature style is wonderfully discursive, ranging from Aristotle through hitting the sack to hitting the bottle of sack, while relishing the rhyme on "Aristotle" and "bottle" along the way; he reminds us again and

again that poetry can be serious without being solemn, that it might even be *fun*.

When the last two cantos of *Don Juan* were published, in March 1824, Byron was in Missolonghi, Greece, where he had gone to help in the Greek war of independence. On the ninth of April he caught a chill; ten days later he was dead. He had never cared to have his "bones mingled with that motley throng" in Poets' Corner—in any case, the Dean of Westminster refused to allow his burial there—and he was laid to rest in his family vault at Hucknall Torckard, Nottinghamshire. In death as in life, Byron set the great example of poet as maverick, joining no club that would have him as a member, at odds with his publisher and public alike—"They hate me, and I detest them, I mean your present public, but they shall not interrupt the march of my mind, nor prevent me from telling the tyrants who are attempting to trample upon all thought that their thrones will yet be rocked to their foundation"—at odds, finally, with himself; as recently as 1938 his tomb was opened for examination and, in the words of one eyewitness, "his right foot had been cut off and lay at the bottom of the coffin."

—PAUL MULDOON

POEMS

From *English Bards and Scotch Reviewers*

Still must I hear?—shall hoarse FITZGERALD BAWL
His creaking couplets in a tavern hall,
And I not sing, lest, haply, Scotch Reviews
Should dub me scribbler, and denounce my Muse?
Prepare for rhyme—I'll publish, right or wrong:
Fools are my theme, let Satire be my song.

When Vice triumphant holds her sov'reign sway,
Obey'd by all, who nought beside obey;
When Folly, frequent harbinger of crime,
Bedecks her cap with bells of every Clime,
When Knaves and Fools combined o'er all prevail,
And weigh their Justice in a Golden Scale,
E'en then the boldest start from public sneers,
Afraid of Shame, unknown to other fears,
More darkly sin, by Satire kept in awe,
And shrink from Ridicule, though not from Law.

Such is the force of Wit! but not belong
To me the arrows of satiric song;
The royal vices of our age demand
A keener weapon, and a mightier hand.
Still there are follies, e'en for me to chase,
And yield at least amusement in the race:

Laugh when I laugh, I seek no other fame,
The cry is up, and scribblers are my game:
Speed Pegasus!—ye strains of great and small,
Ode! Epic! Elegy!—have at you all!
I, too, can scrawl, and once upon a time
I poured along the town a flood of rhyme,
A school-boy freak, unworthy praise or blame;
I printed—older children do the same.
'Tis pleasant, sure, to see one's name in print;
A Book's a Book, altho' there's nothing in't.
Not that a Title's sounding charm can save
Or scrawl or scribbler from an equal grave:
This LAMB must own, since his Patrician name
Failed to preserve the spurious Farce from shame.
No matter, GEORGE continues still to write,
Tho' now the name is veiled from public sight.
Moved by the great example, I pursue
The self-same road, but make my own review:
Not seek great JEFFREY's yet like him will be
Self-constituted Judge of Poesy.

Time was, ere yet in these degenerate days
Ignoble themes obtained mistaken praise,
When Sense and Wit with Poesy allied,
No fabled Graces, flourished side by side,
From the same fount their inspiration drew,
And, reared by Taste, bloomed fairer as they grew.
Then, in this happy Isle, a POPE's pure strain
Sought the rapt soul to charm, nor sought in vain;
A polished nation's praise aspired to claim,
And rais'd the people's, as the poet's fame.
Like him great DRYDEN poured the tide of song,

In stream less smooth indeed, yet doubly strong.
Then Congreve's scenes could cheer, or Otway's melt;
For Nature then an English audience felt—
But why these names, or greater still, retrace,
When all to feebler Bards resign their place?
Yet to such times our lingering looks are cast,
When taste and reason with those times are past.
Now look around, and turn each trifling page,
Survey the precious works that please the age;
This truth at least let Satire's self allow,
No dearth of Bards can be complained of now:
The loaded Press beneath her labour groans,
And Printer's devils shake their weary bones,
While Southey's Epics cram the creaking shelves,
And Little's Lyrics shine in hot-pressed twelves.

. . . .

These are the themes, that claim our plaudits now;
These are the Bards to whom the Muse must bow;
While Milton, Dryden, Pope, alike forgot,
Resign their hallow'd Bays to Walter Scott.

The time has been, when yet the Muse was young,
When Homer swept the lyre, and Maro sung,
An Epic scarce ten centuries could claim,
While awe-struck nations hailed the magic name:
The work of each immortal Bard appears
The single wonder of a thousand years.
Empires have mouldered from the face of earth,
Tongues have expired with those who gave them birth,
Without the glory such a strain can give,
As even in ruin bids the language live.
Not so with us, though minor Bards content,
On one great work a life of labour spent:

With eagle pinion soaring to the skies,
Behold the Ballad-monger SOUTHEY rise!
. . . .
Oh! SOUTHEY, SOUTHEY! cease thy varied song!
A Bard may chaunt too often, and too long:
As thou art strong in verse, in mercy spare!
A fourth, alas! were more than we could bear.
But if, in spite of all the world can say,
Thou still wilt verseward plod thy weary way;
If still in Berkeley-Ballads most uncivil,
Thou wilt devote old women to the devil,
The babe unborn thy dread intent may rue:
"God help thee," SOUTHEY, and thy readers too.

Next comes the dull disciple of thy school,
That mild apostate from poetic rule,
The simple WORDSWORTH, framer of a lay
As soft as evening in his favourite May;
Who warns his friend "to shake off toil and trouble,
And quit his books, for fear of growing double";
Who, both by precept and example, shows
That prose is verse, and verse is merely prose,
Convincing all by demonstration plain,
Poetic souls delight in prose insane;
And Christmas stories tortured into rhyme,
Contain the essence of the true sublime:
Thus when he tells the tale of Betty Foy,
The idiot mother of "an idiot Boy";
A moon-struck silly lad who lost his way,
And, like his Bard, confounded night with day,
So close on each pathetic part he dwells,
And each adventure so sublimely tells,
That all who view the "idiot in his glory,"
Conceive the Bard the hero of the story.

Shall gentle COLERIDGE pass unnoticed here,
To turgid ode, and tumid stanza dear?
Though themes of innocence amuse him best,
Yet still obscurity's a welcome guest.
If inspiration should her aid refuse,
To him who takes a Pixy for a Muse,
Yet none in lofty numbers can surpass
The Bard who soars to elegize an ass:
So well the subject suits his noble mind,
He brays the Laureat of the long-ear'd kind!

. . . .

Thus far I've held my undisturbed career,
Prepared for rancour, steeled 'gainst selfish fear:
This thing of rhyme I ne'er disdained to own,
Though not obtrusive, yet not quite unknown:
My voice was heard again, though not so loud;
My page, though nameless, never disavowed;
And now at once I tear the veil away;—
Cheer on the pack! the Quarry stands at bay,
Unscared by all the din of MELBOURNE house,
By LAMBE's resentment, or by HOLLAND's spouse,
By JEFFREY's harmless pistol, HALLAM's rage,
EDINA's brawny sons and brimstone page.
Our men in buckram shall have blows enough,
And feel, they too are "penetrable stuff":
And though I hope not hence unscathed to go,
Who conquers me, shall find a stubborn foe.
The time hath been, when no harsh sound would fall
From lips that now may seem inbued with gall;
Nor fools nor follies tempt me to despise
The meanest thing that crawled beneath my eyes;
But now, so callous grown, so changed since youth,
I've learned to think, and sternly speak the truth;
Learned to deride the critic's starch decree,

And break him on the wheel he meant for me;
To spurn the rod a scribbler bids me kiss,
Nor care if courts and crowds applaud or hiss:
Nay more, though all my rival rhymesters frown,
I too can hunt a Poetaster down;
And, armed in proof, the gauntlet cast at once
To Scotch marauder, and to Southern dunce.
Thus much I've dared; if my incondite lay
Hath wronged these righteous times let others say;
This, let the world, which knows not how to spare,
Yet rarely blames unjustly, now declare.

The Destruction of Sennacherib

The Assyrian came down like the wolf on the fold,
And his cohorts were gleaming in purple and gold;
And the sheen of their spears was like stars on the sea,
When the blue wave rolls nightly on deep Galilee.

Like the leaves of the forest when Summer is green,
That host with their banners at sunset were seen:
Like the leaves of the forest when Autumn hath blown,
That host on the morrow lay wither'd and strown.

For the Angel of Death spread his wings on the blast,
And breathed in the face of the foe as he pass'd;
And the eyes of the sleepers wax'd deadly and chill,
And their hearts but once heaved, and for ever grew still!

And there lay the steed with his nostril all wide,
But through it there roll'd not the breath of his pride;
And the foam of his gasping lay white on the turf,
And cold as the spray of the rock-beating surf.

And there lay the rider distorted and pale,
With the dew on his brow, and the rust on his mail:
And the tents were all silent, the banners alone,
The lances unlifted, the trumpet unblown.

And the widows of Ashur are loud in their wail,
And the idols are broke in the temple of Baal;
And the might of the Gentile, unsmote by the sword,
Hath melted like snow in the glance of the Lord!

She Walks in Beauty

She walks in beauty, like the night
    Of cloudless climes and starry skies;
And all that's best of dark and bright
    Meet in her aspect and her eyes:
Thus mellowed to that tender light
    Which heaven to gaudy day denies.

One shade the more, one ray the less,
    Had half impaired the nameless grace
Which waves in every raven tress,
    Or softly lightens o'er her face;
Where thoughts serenely sweet express,
    How pure, how dear their dwelling-place.

And on that cheek, and o'er that brow,
    So soft, so calm, yet eloquent,
The smiles that win, the tints that glow,
    But tell of days in goodness spent,
A mind at peace with all below,
    A heart whose love is innocent!

Remember Thee! Remember Thee!

Remember thee! remember thee!
   Till Lethe quench life's burning stream
Remorse and shame shall cling to thee,
   And haunt thee like a feverish dream!

Remember thee! Ay, doubt it not.
   Thy husband too shall think of thee!
By neither shalt thou be forgot,
   Thou *false* to him, thou *fiend* to me!

Written after Swimming from Sestos to Abydos

If, in the month of dark December,
   Leander, who was nightly wont
(What maid will not the tale remember?)
   To cross thy stream, broad Hellespont!

If, when the wintry tempest roar'd,
   He sped to Hero, nothing loth,
And thus of old thy current pour'd,
   Fair Venus! how I pity both!

For *me,* degenerate modern wretch,
   Though in the genial month of May,
My dripping limbs I faintly stretch,
   And think I've done a feat to–day.

But since he cross'd the rapid tide,
   According to the doubtful story,
To woo,—and—Lord knows what beside,
   And swam for Love, as I for Glory;

'Twere hard to say who fared the best:
　　Sad mortals! thus the gods still plague you!
He lost his labour, I my jest;
　　For he was drown'd, and I've the ague.

The Spell is Broke, the Charm is Flown!

Written at Athens, January 16, 1810

The spell is broke, the charm is flown!
　　Thus is it with life's fitful fever:
We madly smile when we should groan:
　　Delirium is our best deceiver.

Each lucid interval of thought
　　Recalls the woes of Nature's charter;
And he that acts as wise men ought,
　　But lives, as saints have died, a martyr.

To Thomas Moore

My boat is on the shore,
　　And my bark is on the sea;
But, before I go, Tom Moore,
　　Here's a double health to thee!

Here's a sigh to those who love me,
　　And a smile to those who hate;
And, whatever sky's above me,
　　Here's a heart for every fate.

Though the ocean roar around me,
  Yet it still shall bear me on;
Though a desert should surround me,
  It hath springs that may be won.

Were't the last drop in the well,
  As I gasp'd upon the brink,
Ere my fainting spirit fell,
  'Tis to thee that I would drink.

With that water, as this wine,
  The libation I would pour
Should be—peace with thine and mine,
  And a health to thee, Tom Moore.

So, We'll Go No More a Roving

So, we'll go no more a roving
  So late into the night,
Though the heart be still as loving,
  And the moon be still as bright.

For the sword outwears its sheath,
  And the soul wears out the breast,
And the heart must pause to breathe,
  And love itself have rest.

Though the night was made for loving,
  And the day returns too soon,
Yet we'll go no more a roving
  By the light of the moon.

Epigrams

ON CASTLEREAGH

1

The world is a bundle of hay,
   Mankind are the asses who pull;
Each tugs it a different way,
   And the greatest of all is John Bull.

2

So Castlereagh has cut his throat!—The worst
Of this is,—that his own was not the first.

3

Oh, Castlereagh! thou art a patriot now;
Cato died for his country, so didst thou:
He perished rather than see Rome enslaved,
Thou cutt'st thy throat that Britain may be saved!

4

Posterity will ne'er survey
   A nobler grave than this:
Here lie the bones of Castlereagh:
   Stop, traveller and——

ON MY WEDDING-DAY
TO PENELOPE

This day, of all our days, has done
   The worst for me and you:—
'Tis just *six* years since we were *one*,
   And *five* since we were *two*.

ON MY THIRTY-THIRD BIRTHDAY
JANUARY 22, 1821

Through life's dull road, so dim and dirty,
I have dragg'd to three-and-thirty.
What have these years left to me?
Nothing—except thirty-three.

Churchill's Grave

A FACT LITERALLY RENDERED

I stood beside the grave of him who blazed
  The comet of a season, and I saw
The humblest of all sepulchres, and gazed
  With not the less of sorrow and of awe
On that neglected turf and quiet stone,
With name no clearer than the names unknown,
Which lay unread around it; and I asked
  The Gardener of that ground, why it might be
That for this plant strangers his memory tasked,
  Through the thick deaths of half a century?
And thus he answered—"Well, I do not know
Why frequent travellers turn to pilgrims so;
He died before my day of Sextonship,
  And I had not the digging of this grave."
And is this all? I thought,—and do we rip
  The veil of Immortality, and crave
I know not what of honour and of light
Through unborn ages, to endure this blight,
So soon, and so successless? As I said,
The Architect of all on which we tread,

For Earth is but a tombstone, did essay
To extricate remembrance from the clay,
Whose minglings might confuse a Newton's thought
  Were it not that all life must end in one,
Of which we are but dreamers;—as he caught
  As 'twere the twilight of a former Sun,
Thus spoke he,—"I believe the man of whom
You wot, who lies in this selected tomb,
Was a most famous writer in his day,
And therefore travellers step from out their way
To pay him honour,—and myself whate'er
  Your honour pleases:"—then most pleased I shook
  From out my pocket's avaricious nook
Some certain coins of silver, which as 'twere
Perforce I gave this man, though I could spare
So much but inconveniently:—Ye smile,
I see ye, ye profane ones! all the while,
Because my homely phrase the truth would tell.
You are the fools, not I—for I did dwell
With a deep thought, and with a softened eye,
On that Old Sexton's natural homily,
In which there was Obscurity and Fame,—
The Glory and the Nothing of a Name.

Diodati, 1816

Epistle to Augusta

My sister! my sweet sister! if a name
Dearer and purer were, it should be thine.
Mountains and seas divide us, but I claim
No tears, but tenderness to answer mine:
Go where I will, to me thou art the same—

A loved regret which I would not resign.
There yet are two things in my destiny,—
A world to roam through, and a home with thee.

The first were nothing—had I still the last,
It were the haven of my happiness;
But other claims and other ties thou hast,
And mine is not the wish to make them less.
A strange doom is thy father's son's, and past
Recalling, as it lies beyond redress;
Reversed for him our grandsire's fate of yore,—
He had no rest at sea, nor I on shore.

If my inheritance of storms hath been
In other elements, and on the rocks
Of perils, overlooked or unforeseen,
I have sustained my share of worldly shocks,
The fault was mine; nor do I seek to screen
My errors with defensive paradox;
I have been cunning in mine overthrow,
The careful pilot of my proper woe.

Mine were my faults, and mine be their reward.
My whole life was a contest, since the day
That gave me being, gave me that which marred
The gift,—a fate, or will, that walked astray;
And I at times have found the struggle hard,
And thought of shaking off my bonds of clay:
But now I fain would for a time survive,
If but to see what next can well arrive.

Kingdoms and empires in my little day
I have outlived, and yet I am not old;

And when I look on this, the petty spray
Of my own years of trouble, which have rolled
Like a wild bay of breakers, melts away:
Something—I know not what—does still uphold
A spirit of slight patience;—not in vain,
Even for its own sake, do we purchase pain.

Perhaps the workings of defiance stir
Within me—or perhaps a cold despair,
Brought on when ills habitually recur,—
Perhaps a kinder clime, or purer air,
(For even to this may change of soul refer,
And with light armour we may learn to bear,)
Have taught me a strange quiet, which was not
The chief companion of a calmer lot.

I feel almost at times as I have felt
In happy childhood; trees, and flowers, and brooks,
Which do remember me of where I dwelt
Ere my young mind was sacrificed to books,
Come as of yore upon me, and can melt
My heart with recognition of their looks;
And even at moments I could think I see
Some living things to love—but none like thee.

Here are the Alpine landscapes which create
A fund for contemplation;—to admire
Is a brief feeling of a trivial date;
But something worthier do such scenes inspire:
Here to be lonely is not desolate,
For much I view which I could most desire,
And, above all, a lake I can behold
Lovelier, not dearer, than our own of old.

Oh that thou wert but with me!—but I grow
The fool of my own wishes, and forget
The solitude which I have vaunted so
Has lost its praise in this but one regret;
There may be others which I less may show;—
I am not of the plaintive mood, and yet
I feel an ebb in my philosophy,
And the tide rising in my altered eye.

I did remind thee of our own dear Lake,
By the old Hall which may be mine no more.
Leman's is fair; but think not I forsake
The sweet remembrance of a dearer shore:
Sad havoc Time must with my memory make,
Ere *that* or *thou* can fade these eyes before;
Though, like all things which I have loved, they are
Resigned for ever, or divided far.

The world is all before me; I but ask
Of Nature that with which she will comply—
It is but in her summer's sun to bask,
To mingle with the quiet of her sky,
To see her gentle face without a mask,
And never gaze on it with apathy.
She was my early friend, and now shall be
My sister—till I look again on thee.

I can reduce all feelings but this one;
And that I would not;—for at length I see
Such scenes as those wherein my life begun.
The earliest—even the only paths for me—
Had I but sooner learnt the crowd to shun,
I had been better than I now can be;

The passions which have torn me would have slept;
I had not suffered, and *thou* hadst not wept.

With false Ambition what had I to do?
Little with Love, and least of all with Fame;
And yet they came unsought, and with me grew,
And made me all which they can make—a name.
Yet this was not the end I did pursue;
Surely I once beheld a nobler aim.
But all is over—I am one the more
To baffled millions which have gone before.

And for the future, this world's future may
From me demand but little of my care;
I have outlived myself by many a day;
Having survived so many things that were;
My years have been no slumber, but the prey
Of ceaseless vigils; for I had the share
Of life which might have filled a century,
Before its fourth in time had passed me by.

And for the remnant which may be to come
I am content; and for the past I feel
Not thankless,—for within the crowded sum
Of struggles, happiness at times would steal,
And for the present, I would not benumb
My feelings farther.—Nor shall I conceal
That with all this I still can look around,
And worship Nature with a thought profound.

For thee, my own sweet sister, in thy heart
I know myself secure, as thou in mine;
We were and are—I am, even as thou art—

Beings who ne'er each other can resign;
It is the same, together or apart,
From life's commencement to its slow decline
We are entwined—let death come slow or fast,
The tie which bound the first endures the last!

Lines on Hearing that Lady Byron was Ill

And thou wert sad—yet I was not with thee;
And thou wert sick, and yet I was not near;
Methought that joy and health alone could be
Where I was *not*—and pain and sorrow here!
And is it thus?—it is as I foretold,
And shall be more so; for the mind recoils
Upon itself, and the wrecked heart lies cold,
While heaviness collects the shattered spoils.
It is not in the storm nor in the strife
We feel benumbed, and wish to be no more,
But in the after-silence on the shore,
When all is lost, except a little life.

I am too well avenged!—but 'twas my right;
Whate'er my sins might be, *thou* wert not sent
To be the Nemesis who should requite—
Nor did Heaven choose so near an instrument.
Mercy is for the merciful!—if thou
Hast been of such, 'twill be accorded now.
Thy nights are banished from the realms of sleep.—
Yes! they may flatter thee, but thou shalt feel
A hollow agony which will not heal,
For thou art pillowed on a course too deep;
Thou hast sown in my sorrow, and must reap
The bitter harvest in a woe as real!

I have had many foes, but none like thee;
   For 'gainst the rest myself I could defend,
   And be avenged, or turn them into friend;
But thou in safe implacability
Hadst nought to dread—in thy own weakness shielded,
And in my love, which hath but too much yielded,
   And spared, for thy sake, some I should not spare;
And thus upon the world—trust in thy truth,
And the wild fame of my ungoverned youth—
   On things that were not, and on things that are—
Even upon such a basis hast thou built
A monument, whose cement hath been guilt!
   The moral Clytemnestra of thy lord,
   And hewed down, with an unsuspected sword,
Fame, peace, and hope—and all the better life
   Which, but for this cold treason of thy heart,
Might still have risen from out the grave of strife,
   And found a nobler duty than to part.
But of thy virtues didst thou make a vice,
   Trafficking with them in a purpose cold,
   For present anger, and for future gold—
And buying other's grief at any price.
And thus once entered into crooked ways,
The early truth, which was thy proper praise,
Did not still walk beside thee—but at times,
And with a breast unknowing its own crimes,
Deceit, averments incompatible,
Equivocations, and the thoughts which dwell
   In Janus-spirits—the significant eye
Which learns to lie with silence—the pretext
Of prudence, with advantages annexed—
The acquiescence in all things which tend,
No matter how, to the desired end—
   All found a place in thy philosophy.

The means were worthy, and the end is won—
I would not do by thee as thou hast done!

September, 1816

On This Day I Complete My Thirty-sixth Year

Missolonghi, Jan. 22nd, 1824

'Tis time this heart should be unmoved,
    Since others it hath ceased to move:
Yet, though I cannot be beloved,
        Still let me love!

My days are in the yellow leaf;
    The flowers and fruits of love are gone;
The worm, the canker, and the grief
        Are mine alone!

The fire that on my bosom preys
    Is lone as some volcanic isle;
No torch is kindled at its blaze—
        A funeral pile.

The hope, the fear, the jealous care,
    The exalted portion of the pain
And power of love, cannot share,
        But wear the chain.

But 'tis not *thus*—and 'tis not *here*—
    Such thoughts should shake my soul, nor *now*
Where glory decks the hero's bier,
        Or binds his brow.

The sword, the banner, and the field,
   Glory and Greece, around me see!
The Spartan, borne upon his shield,
      Was not more free.

Awake! (not Greece—she *is* awake!)
   Awake, my spirit! Think through *whom*
Thy life-blood tracks its parent lake,
      And then strike home!

Tread those reviving passions down,
   Unworthy manhood!—unto thee
Indifferent should the smile or frown
      Of beauty be.

If thou regret'st thy youth, *why live?*
   The land of honourable death
Is here:—up to the field, and give
      Away thy breath!

Seek out—less often sought than found—
   A soldier's grave, for thee the best;
Then look around, and choose thy ground,
      And take thy rest.

Beppo

'Tis known, at least it should be, that throughout
   All countries of the Catholic persuasion,
Some weeks before Shrove Tuesday comes about,
   The people take their fill of recreation,

And buy repentance, ere they grow devout,
    However high their rank, or low their station,
With fiddling, feasting, dancing, drinking, masquing,
And other things which may be had for asking.

The moment night with dusky mantle covers
    The skies (and the more duskily the better),
The times less liked by husbands than by lovers
    Begins, and prudery flings aside her fetter;
And gaiety on restless tiptoe hovers,
    Giggling with all the gallants who beset her;
And there are songs and quavers, roaring, humming,
Guitars, and every other sort of strumming.

And there are dresses splendid, but fantastical,
    Masks of all times and nations, Turks and Jews,
And harlequins and clowns, with feats gymnastical,
    Greeks, Romans, Yankee-doodles, and Hindoos;
All kinds of dress, except the ecclesiastical,
    All people, as their fancies hit, may choose,
But no one in these parts may quiz the clergy,—
Therefore take heed, ye Freethinkers! I charge ye.

You'd better walk about begirt with briars,
    Instead of coat and smallclothes, than put on
A single stitch reflecting upon friars,
    Although you swore it only was in fun;
They'd haul you o'er the coals, and stir the fires
    Of Phlegethon with every mother's son,
Nor say one mass to cool the caldron's bubble
That boiled your bones, unless you paid them double.

But saving this, you may put on whate'er
    You like by way of doublet, cape or cloak,

Such as in Monmouth-street, or in Rag Fair,
    Would rig you out in seriousness or joke;
And even in Italy such places are,
    With prettier name in softer accents spoke,
For, bating Covent Garden, I can hit on
No place that's called "Piazza" in Great Britain.

This feast is named the Carnival, which being
    Interpreted, implies "farewell to flesh":
So called, because the name and thing agreeing,
    Through Lent they live on fish both salt and fresh.
But why they usher Lent with so much glee in,
    Is more than I can tell, although I guess
'Tis as we take a glass with friends at parting,
In the stage-coach or packet just at starting.

And thus they bid farewell to carnal dishes,
    And solid meats, and highly spiced ragouts,
To live for forty days on ill-dressed fishes,
    Because they have no sauces to their stews;
A thing which causes many "poohs" and "pishes,"
    And several oaths (which would not suit the Muse),
From travellers accustomed from a boy
To eat their salmon, at the least, with soy;

And therefore humbly I would recommend
    "The curious in fish-sauce," before they cross
The sea, to bid their cook, or wife, or friend,
    Walk or ride to the Strand, and buy in gross
(Or if set out beforehand, these may send
    By any means least liable to loss),
Ketchup, Soy, Chili-vinegar, and Harvey,
Or, by the Lord! a Lent will well nigh starve ye;

That is to say, if your religion's Roman,
  And you at Rome would do as Romans do,
According to the proverb,—although no man,
  If foreign, is obliged to fast; and you,
If Protestant, or sickly, or a woman,
  Would rather dine in sin on a ragout—
Dine and be d——d! I don't mean to be coarse,
But that's the penalty, to say no worse.

Of all the places where the Carnival
  Was most facetious in the days of yore,
For dance, and song, and serenade, and ball,
  And masque, and mime, and mystery, and more
Than I have time to tell now, or at all,
  Venice the bell from every city bore,—
And at the moment when I fix my story,
That sea-born city was in all her glory.

They've pretty faces yet, those same Venetians,
  Black eyes, arched brows, and sweet expressions still;
Such as of old were copied from the Grecians,
  In ancient arts by moderns mimicked ill;
And like so many Venuses of Titian's
  (The best's at Florence—see it, if ye will,)
They look when leaning over the balcony,
Or stepped from out a picture by Giorgione,

Whose tints are truth and beauty at their best;
  And when you to Manfrini's palace go,
That picture (howsoever fine the rest)
  Is loveliest to my mind of all the show;
It may perhaps be also to *your* zest,
  And that's the cause I rhyme upon it so:

'Tis but a portrait of his son, and wife,
And self; but *such* a woman! love in life!

Love in full life and length, not love ideal,
    No, nor ideal beauty, that fine name,
But something better still, so very real,
    That the sweet model must have been the same;
A thing that you would purchase, beg, or steal,
    Wer't not impossible, besides a shame:
The face recalls some face, as 'twere with pain,
You once have seen, but ne'er will see again;

One of those forms which flit by us, when we
    Are young, and fix our eyes on every face;
And, oh! the loveliness at times we see
    In momentary gliding, the soft grace,
The youth, the bloom, the beauty which agree,
    In many a nameless being we retrace,
Whose course and home we knew not, nor shall know,
Like the lost Pleiad seen no more below.

I said that like a picture by Giorgione
    Venetian women were, and so they *are,*
Particularly seen from a balcony,
    (For beauty's sometimes best set off afar)
And there, just like a heroine of Goldoni,
    They peep from out the blind, or o'er the bar;
And truth to say, they're mostly very pretty,
And rather like to show it, more's the pity!

For glances beget ogles, ogles sighs,
    Sighs wishes, wishes words, and words a letter,
Which flies on wings of light-heeled Mercuries,

Who do such things because they know no better;
And then, God knows what mischief may arise,
When love links two young people in one fetter,
Vile assignations, and adulterous beds,
Elopements, broken vows, and hearts, and heads.

Shakespeare described the sex in Desdemona
As very fair, but yet suspect in fame,
And to this day from Venice to Verona
Such matters may be probably the same,
Except that since those times was never known a
Husband whom mere suspicion could inflame
To suffocate a wife no more than twenty,
Because she had a "cavalier servente."

Their jealousy (if they are ever jealous)
Is of a fair complexion altogether,
Not like that sooty devil of Othello's,
Which smothers women in a bed of feather,
But worthier of these much more jolly fellows,
When weary of the matrimonial tether
His head for such a wife no mortal bothers,
But takes at once another, or another's.

Didst ever see a Gondola? For fear
You should not, I'll describe it you exactly:
'Tis a long covered boat that's common here,
Carved at the prow, built lightly, but compactly,
Rowed by two rowers, each called "Gondolier,"
It glides along the water looking blackly,
Just like a coffin clapt in a canoe,
Where none can make out what you say or do.

And up and down the long canals they go,
    And under the Rialto shoot along,
By night and day, all paces, swift or slow,
    And round the theatres, a sable throng,
They wait in their dusk livery of woe,—
    But not to them do woeful things belong,
For sometimes they contain a deal of fun,
Like mourning coaches when the funeral's done.

But to my story.—'Twas some years ago,
    It may be thirty, forty, more or less,
The Carnival was at its height, and so
    Were all kinds of buffoonery and dress;
A certain lady went to see the show,
    Her real name I know not, nor can guess,
And so we'll call her Laura, if you please,
Because it slips into my verse with ease.

She was not old, nor young, nor at the years
    Which certain people call a *"certain age,"*
Which yet the most uncertain age appears,
    Because I never heard, nor could engage
A person yet by prayers, or bribes, or tears,
    To name, define by speech, or write on page,
The period meant precisely by that word,—
Which surely is exceedingly absurd.

Laura was blooming still, had made the best
    Of time, and time returned the compliment,
And treated her genteelly, so that, dressed,
    She looked extremely well where'er she went;
A pretty woman is a welcome guest,
    And Laura's brow a frown had rarely bent;

Indeed, she shone all smiles, and seemed to flatter
Mankind with her black eyes for looking at her.

She was a married women; 'tis convenient,
   Because in Christian countries 'tis a rule
To view their little slips with eyes more lenient;
   Whereas if single ladies play the fool,
(Unless within the period intervenient
   A well-timed wedding makes the scandal cool)
I don't know how they ever can get over it,
Except they manage never to discover it.

Her husband sailed upon the Adriatic,
   And made some voyages, too, in other seas,
And when he lay in quarantine for pratique
   (A forty days' precaution 'gainst disease),
His wife would mount, at times, her highest attic,
   For thence she could discern the ship with ease:
He was a merchant trading to Aleppo,
His name Giuseppe, called more briefly, Beppo.

He was a man as dusky as a Spaniard,
   Sunburnt with travel, yet a portly figure;
Though coloured, as it were, within a tanyard,
   He was a person both of sense and vigour—
A better seaman never yet did man yard;
   And she, although her manners showed no rigour,
Was deemed a woman of the strictest principle,
So much as to be thought almost invincible.

But several years elapsed since they had met;
   Some people thought the ship was lost, and some
That he had somehow blundered into debt,
   And did not like the thought of steering home;

And there were several offered any bet,
   Or that he would, or that he would not come;
For most men (till by losing rendered sager)
Will back their own opinions with a wager.

'Tis said that their last parting was pathetic,
   As partings often are, or ought to be,
And their presentiment was quite prophetic,
   That they should never more each other see,
(A sort of morbid feeling, half poetic,
   Which I have known occur in two or three,)
When kneeling on the shore upon her sad knee
He left this Adriatic Ariadne.

And Laura waited long, and wept a little,
   And thought of wearing weeds, as well she might;
She almost lost all appetite for victual,
   And could not sleep with ease alone at night;
She deemed the window-frames and shutters brittle
   Against a daring housebreaker or sprite,
And so she thought it prudent to connect her
With a vice-husband, *chiefly to protect her.*

She chose, (and what is there they will not choose,
   If only you will but oppose their choice?)
Till Beppo should return from his long cruise,
   And bid once more her faithful heart rejoice,
A man some women like, and yet abuse—
   A coxcomb was he by the public voice;
A Count of wealth, they said, as well as quality,
And in his pleasures of great liberality.

And then he was a Count, and then he knew
   Music, and dancing, fiddling, French and Tuscan;

The last not easy, be it known to you,
   For few Italians speak the right Etruscan.
He was a critic upon operas, too,
   And knew all niceties of sock and buskin;
And no Venetian audience could endure a
Song, scene, or air, when he cried "seccatura!"

His "bravo" was decisive, for that sound
   Hushed "Academie" sighed in silent awe;
The fiddlers trembled as he looked around,
   For fear of some false note's detected flaw;
The "prima donna's" tuneful heart would bound,
   Dreading the deep damnation of his "bah!"
Soprano, basso, even the contra-alto,
Wished him five fathom under the Rialto.

He patronised the Improvisatori,
   Nay, could himself extemporise some stanzas,
Wrote rhymes, sang songs, could also tell a story,
   Sold pictures, and was skilful in the dance as
Italians can be, though in this their glory
   Must surely yield the palm to that which France has;
In short, he was a perfect cavaliero,
And to his very valet seemed a hero.

Then he was faithful too, as well as amorous;
   So that no sort of female could complain,
Although they're now and then a little clamorous,
   He never put the pretty souls in pain;
His heart was one of those which most enamour us,
   Wax to receive, and marble to retain:
He was a lover of the good old school,
Who still become more constant as they cool.

No wonder such accomplishments should turn
   A female head, however sage and steady—
With scarce a hope that Beppo could return,
   In law he was almost as good as dead, he
Nor sent, nor wrote, nor showed the least concern,
   And she had waited several years already;
And really if a man won't let us know
That he's alive, he's *dead,* or should be so.

Besides, within the Alps, to every woman,
   (Although, God knows, it is a grievous sin,)
'Tis, I may say, permitted to have *two* men;
   I can't tell who first brought the custom in,
But "Cavalier Serventes" are quite common,
   And no one notices nor cares a pin;
And we may call this (not to say the worst)
A *second* marriage which corrupts the *first.*

The word was formerly a "Cicisbeo,"
   But *that* is now grown vulgar and indecent;
The Spaniards call the person a *"Cortejo,"*
   For the same mode subsists in Spain, though recent;
In short it reaches from the Po to Teio,
   And may perhaps at last be o'er the sea sent:
But Heaven preserve Old England from such courses!
Or what becomes of damage and divorces?

However, I still think, with all due deference
   To the fair *single* part of the creation,
That married ladies should preserve the preference
   In *tête à tête* or general conversation—
And this I say without peculiar reference
   To England, France, or any other nation—

Because they know the world, and are at ease,
And being natural, naturally please.

'Tis true, your budding Miss is very charming,
   But shy and awkward at first coming out,
So much alarmed, that she is quite alarming,
   All Giggle, Blush; half Pertness, and half Pout;
And glancing at *Mamma,* for fear there's harm in
   What you, she, it, or they, may be about,
The Nursery still lisps out in all they utter—
Besides, they always smell of bread and butter.

But "Cavalier Servente" is the phrase
   Used in politest circles to express
This supernumerary slave, who stays
   Close to the lady as a part of dress,
Her word the only law which he obeys.
   His is no sinecure, as you may guess;
Coach, servants, gondola, he goes to call,
And carries fan and tippet, gloves and shawl.

With all its sinful doings, I must say,
   That Italy's a pleasant place to me,
Who love to see the Sun shine every day,
   And vines (not nailed to walls) from tree to tree
Festooned, much like the back scene of a play,
   Or melodrame, which people flock to see,
When the first act is ended by a dance
In vineyards copied from the south of France.

I like on Autumn evenings to ride out,
   Without being forced to bid my groom be sure
My cloak is round his middle strapped about,
   Because the skies are not the most secure;

I know too that, if stopped upon my route,
　　Where the green alleys windingly allure,
Reeling with grapes red wagons choke the way,—
In England 'twould be dung, dust, or a dray.

I also like to dine on becaficas,
　　To see the Sun set, sure he'll rise to-morrow,
Not through a misty morning twinkling weak as
　　A drunken man's dead eye in maudlin sorrow,
But with all Heaven t'himself; the day will break as
　　Beauteous as cloudless, nor be forced to borrow
That sort of farthing candlelight which glimmers
Where reeking London's smoky cauldron simmers.

I love the language, that soft bastard Latin,
　　Which melts like kisses from a female mouth,
And sounds as if it should be writ on satin,
　　With syllables which breathe of the sweet South,
And gentle liquids gliding all so pat in,
　　That not a single accent seems uncouth,
Like our harsh northern whistling, grunting guttural,
Which we're obliged to hiss, and spit, and splutter all.

I like the women too (forgive my folly),
　　From the rich peasant cheek of ruddy bronze,
And large black eyes that flash on you a volley
　　Of rays that say a thousand things at once,
To the high dama's brow, more melancholy,
　　But clear, and with a wild and liquid glance,
Heart on her lips, and soul within her eyes,
Soft as her clime, and sunny as her skies.

Eve of the land which still is Paradise!
　　Italian beauty didst thou not inspire

Raphael, who died in thy embrace, and vies
    With all we know of Heaven, or can desire,
In what he hath bequeathed us?—in what guise,
    Though flashing from the fervour of the lyre,
Would *words* describe thy past and present glow,
While yet Canova can create below?

"England! with all thy faults I love thee still,"
    I said at Calais, and have not forgot it;
I like to speak and lucubrate my fill;
    I like the government (but that is not it);
I like the freedom of the press and quill;
    I like the Habeas Corpus (when we've got it)
I like a parliamentary debate,
Particularly when 'tis not too late;

I like the taxes, when they're not too many
    I like a seacoal fire, when not too dear;
I like a beef-steak, too, as well as any;
    Have no objection to a pot of beer;
I like the weather when it is not rainy,
    That is, I like two months of every year.
And so God save the Regent, Church, and King!
Which means that I like all and every thing.

Our standing army, and disbanded seamen,
    Poor's rate, Reform, my own, the nation's debt,
Our little riots just to show we're free men,
    Our trifling bankruptcies in the Gazette,
Our cloudy climate, and our chilly women,
    All these I can forgive, and those forget,
And greatly venerate our recent glories,
And wish they were not owing to the Tories.

But to my tale of Laura,—for I find
    Digression is a sin, that by degrees
Becomes exceeding tedious to my mind,
    And, therefore, may the reader too displease—
The gentle reader, who may wax unkind,
    And caring little for the author's ease,
Insist on knowing what he means, a hard
And hapless situation for a bard.

Oh that I had the art of easy writing
    What should be easy reading! could I scale
Parnassus, where the Muses sit inditing
    Those pretty poems never known to fail,
How quickly would I print (the world delighting)
    A Grecian, Syrian, or Assyrian tale;
And sell you, mixed with western sentimentalism,
Some samples of the finest Orientalism.

But I am but a nameless sort of person,
    (A broken Dandy lately on my travels)
And take for rhyme, to hook my rambling verse on,
    The first that Walker's Lexicon unravels,
And when I can't find that, I put a worse on,
    Not caring as I ought for critics' cavils;
I've half a mind to tumble down to prose,
But verse is more in fashion—so here goes.

The Count and Laura made their new arrangement,
    Which lasted, as arrangements sometimes do,
For half a dozen years without estrangement;
    They had their little differences, too;
Those jealous whiffs, which never any change meant;
    In such affairs there probably are few

Who have not had this pouting sort of squabble,
From sinners of high station to the rabble.

But, on the whole, they were a happy pair,
    As happy as unlawful love could make them;
The gentleman was fond, the lady fair,
    Their chains so slight, 'twas not worth while to break them:
The world beheld them with indulgent air;
    The pious only wished "the devil take them!"
He took them not; he very often waits,
And leaves old sinners to be young ones' baits.

But they were young: Oh! what without our youth
    Would love be! What would youth be without love!
Youth lends its joy, and sweetness, vigour, truth,
    Heart, soul, and all that seems as from above;
But, languishing with years, it grows uncouth—
    One of few things experience don't improve,
Which is, perhaps, the reason why old fellows
Are always so preposterously jealous.

It was the Carnival, as I have said
    Some six and thirty stanzas back, and so
Laura the usual preparations made,
    Which you do when your mind's made up to go
To-night to Mrs. Boehm's masquerade,
    Spectator, or partaker in the show;
The only difference known between the cases
Is—*here,* we have six weeks of "varnished faces."

Laura, when dressed, was (as I sang before)
    A pretty woman as was ever seen,
Fresh as the Angel o'er a new inn door,
    Or frontispiece of a new Magazine,

With all the fashions which the last month wore,
  Coloured, and silver paper leaved between
That and the title-page, for fear the press
Should soil with parts of speech the parts of dress.

They went to the Ridotto;—'tis a hall
  Where people dance, and sup, and dance again;
Its proper name, perhaps, were a masqued ball,
  But that's of no importance to my strain;
'Tis (on a smaller scale) like our Vauxhall,
  Excepting that it can't be spoilt by rain;
The company is "mixed" (the phrase I quote is
As much as saying, they're below your notice);

For a "mixed company" implies that, save
  Yourself and friends, and half a hundred more,
Whom you may bow to without looking grave,
  The rest are but a vulgar set, the bore
Of public places, where they basely brave
  The fashionable stare of twenty score
Of well-bred persons, called *"The World"*; but I,
Although I know them, really don't know why.

This is the case in England; at least was
  During the dynasty of Dandies, now
Perchance succeeded by some other class
  Of imitated imitators:—how
Irreparably soon decline, alas!
  The demagogues of fashion: all below
Is frail; how easily the world is lost
By love, or war, and now and then by frost!

Crushed was Napoleon by the northern Thor,
  Who knocked his army down with icy hammer,

Stopped by the *elements,* like a whaler, or
    A blundering novice in his new French grammar;
Good cause had he to doubt the chance of war,
    And as for Fortune—but I dare not d——n her,
Because, were I to ponder to infinity,
The more I should believe in her divinity.

She rules the present, past, and all to be yet,
    She gives us luck in lotteries, love and marriage;
I cannot say that she's done much for me yet;
    Not that I mean her bounties to disparage,
We've not yet closed accounts, and we shall see yet
    How much she'll make amends for past miscarriage;
Meantime the Goddess I'll no more importune,
Unless to thank her when she's made my fortune.

To turn,—and to return;—the devil take it!
    This story slips for ever through my fingers,
Because, just as the stanza likes to make it,
    It needs must be—and so it rather lingers;
This form of verse began, I can't well break it,
    But must keep time and tune like public singers;
But if I once get through my present measure,
I'll take another when I'm next at leisure.

They went to the Ridotto ('tis a place
    To which I mean to go myself to-morrow,
Just to divert my thoughts a little space
    Because I'm rather hippish, and may borrow
Some spirits, guessing at what kind of face
    May lurk beneath each mask; and as my sorrow
Slackens its pace sometimes, I'll make, or find,
Something shall leave it half an hour behind.)

Now Laura moves along the joyous crowd,
   Smiles in her eyes, and simpers on her lips;
To some she whispers, others speaks aloud;
   To some she curtsies, and to some she dips,
Complains of warmth, and this complaint avowed,
   Her lover brings the lemonade, she sips;
She then surveys, condemns, but pities still
Her dearest friends for being dressed so ill.

One has false curls, another too much paint,
   A third—where did she buy that frightful turban?
A fourth's so pale she fears she's going to faint,
   A fifth's look's vulgar, dowdyish, and suburban,
A sixth's white silk has got a yellow taint,
   A seventh's thin muslin surely will be her bane,
And lo! an eighth appears,—"I'll see no more!"
For fear, like Banquo's kings, they reach a score.

Meantime, while she was thus at others gazing,
   Others were levelling their looks at her;
She heard the men's half-whispered mode of praising,
   And, till 'twas done, determined not to stir;
The women only thought it quite amazing
   That, at her time of life, so many were
Admirers still,—but men are so debased,
Those brazen creatures always suit their taste.

For my part, now, I ne'er could understand
   Why naughty women—but I won't discuss
A thing which is a scandal to the land,
   I only don't see why it should be thus;
And if I were but in a gown and band,
   Just to entitle me to make a fuss,

I'd preach on this till Wilberforce and Romilly
Should quote in their next speeches from my homily.

While Laura thus was seen, and seeing, smiling,
    Talking, she knew not why, and cared not what,
So that her female friends, with envy broiling,
    Beheld her airs and triumph, and all that;
And well-dressed males still kept before her filing,
    And passing bowed and mingled with her chat;
More than the rest one person seemed to stare
With pertinacity that's rather rare.

He was a Turk, the colour of mahogany;
    And Laura saw him, and at first was glad,
Because the Turks so much admire philogyny,
    Although their usage of their wives is sad;
'Tis said they use no better than a dog any
    Poor woman, whom they purchase like a pad:
They have a number, though they ne'er exhibit 'em,
Four wives by law, and concubines "ad libitum."

They lock them up, and veil, and guard them daily,
    They scarcely can behold their male relations,
So that their moments do not pass so gaily
    As is supposed the case with northern nations;
Confinement, too, must make them look quite palely;
    And as the Turks abhor long conversations,
Their days are either passed in doing nothing,
Or bathing, nursing, making love, and clothing.

They cannot read, and so don't lisp in criticism;
    Nor write, and so they don't affect the muse;
Were never caught in epigram or witticism,
    Have no romances, sermons, plays, reviews,—

In harams learning soon would make a pretty schism,
  But luckily these beauties are no "Blues";
No bustling Botherbys have they to show 'em
"That charming passage in the last new poem":

No solemn, antique gentleman of rhyme,
  Who having angled all his life for fame,
And getting but a nibble at a time,
  Still fussily keeps fishing on, the same
Small "Triton of the minnows," the sublime
  Of mediocrity, the furious tame,
The echo's echo, usher of the school
Of female wits, boy bards—in short, a fool!

A stalking oracle of awful phrase,
  The approving *"Good!"* (by no means GOOD in law)
Humming like flies around the newest blaze,
  The bluest of bluebottles you e'er saw,
Teasing with blame, excruciating with praise,
  Gorging the little fame he gets all raw,
Translating tongues he knows not even by letter,
And sweating plays so middling, bad were better.

One hates an author that's *all author,* fellows
  In foolscap uniforms turned up with ink,
So very anxious, clever, fine, and jealous,
  One don't know what to say to them, or think,
Unless to puff them with a pair of bellows;
  Of coxcombry's worst coxcombs e'en the pink
Are preferable to these shreds of paper,
These unquenched snuffings of the midnight taper.

Of these same we see several, and of others,
  Men of the world, who know the world like men,

Scott, Rogers, Moore, and all the better brothers,
    Who think of something else besides the pen;
But for the children of the "mighty mother's,"
    The would-be wits, and can't-be gentlemen,
I leave them to their daily "tea is ready,"
Smug coterie, and literary lady.

The poor dear Mussulwomen whom I mention
    Have none of these instructive pleasant people,
And *one* would seem to them a new invention,
    Unknown as bells within a Turkish steeple;
I think 'twould almost be worth while to pension
    (Though best-sown projects very often reap ill)
A missionary author, just to preach
Our Christian usage of the parts of speech.

No chemistry for them unfolds her gases,
    No metaphysics are let loose in lectures,
No circulating library amasses
    Religious novels, moral tales, and strictures
Upon the living manners, as they pass us;
    No exhibition glares with annual pictures;
They stare not on the stars from out their attics,
Nor deal (thank God for that!) in mathematics.

Why I thank God for that is no great matter,
    I have my reasons, you no doubt suppose,
And as, perhaps, they would not highly flatter,
    I'll keep them for my life (to come) in prose;
I fear I have a little turn for satire,
    And yet methinks the older that one grows
Inclines us more to laugh than scold, though laughter
Leaves us so doubly serious shortly after.

Oh, mirth and innocence! Oh, milk and water!
  Ye happy mixtures of more happy days!
In these sad centuries of sin and slaughter,
  Abominable Man no more allays
His thirst with such pure beverage. No matter,
  I love you both, and both shall have my praise:
Oh, for old Saturn's reign of sugar-candy!—
Meantime I drink to your return in brandy.

Our Laura's Turk still kept his eyes upon her,
  Less in the Mussulman than Christian way,
Which seems to say, "Madam, do I you honour,
  "And while I please to stare, you'll please to stay."
Could staring win a woman, this had won her,
  But Laura could not thus be led astray;
She had stood fire too long and well, to boggle
Even at this stranger's most outlandish ogle.

The morning now was on the point of breaking,
  A turn of time at which I would advise
Ladies who have been dancing, or partaking
  In any other kind of exercise,
To make their preparations for forsaking
  The ball-room ere the sun begins to rise,
Because when once the lamps and candles fail,
His blushes make them look a little pale.

I've seen some balls and revels in my time,
  And stayed them over for some silly reason,
And then I looked (I hope it was no crime)
  To see what lady best stood out the season;
And though I've seen some thousands in their prime,
  Lovely and pleasing, and who still may please on,

I never saw but one (the stars withdrawn)
Whose bloom could after dancing dare the dawn.

The name of this Aurora I'll not mention,
   Although I might, for she was nought to me
More than that patent work of God's invention,
   A charming woman, whom we like to see;
But writing names would merit reprehension,
   Yet if you like to find out this fair *she,*
At the next London or Parisian ball
You still may mark her cheek, out-blooming all.

Laura, who knew it would not do at all
   To meet the daylight after seven hours' sitting
Among three thousand people at a ball,
   To make her curtsy thought it right and fitting;
The Count was at her elbow with her shawl,
   And they the room were on the point of quitting,
When lo! those cursed gondoliers had got
Just in the very place where they *should not.*

In this they're like our coachmen, and the cause
   Is much the same—the crowd, and pulling, hauling,
With blasphemies enough to break their jaws,
   They make a never intermitted bawling.
At home, our Bow-street gemmem keep the laws,
   And here a sentry stands within your calling;
But for all that, there is a deal of swearing,
And nauseous words past mentioning or bearing.

The Count and Laura found their boat at last,
   And homeward floated o'er the silent tide,
Discussing all the dances gone and past;
   The dancers and their dresses, too, besides;

Some little scandals eke; but all aghast
   (As to their palace-stairs the rowers glide)
Sate Laura by the side of her Adorer,
When lo! the Mussulman was there before her.

"Sir," said the Count, with brow exceeding grave,
   "Your unexpected presence here will make
It necessary for myself to crave
   Its import? But perhaps 'tis a mistake;
I hope it is so; and, at once to waive
   All compliment, I hope so for *your* sake;
You understand my meaning, or you *shall*."
"Sir," (quoth the Turk) " 'tis no mistake at all:

"That lady is *my wife!*" Much wonder paints
   The lady's changing cheek, as well it might;
But where an Englishwoman sometimes faints,
   Italian females don't do so outright;
They only call a little on their saints,
   And then come to themselves, almost or quite;
Which saves much hartshorn, salts, and sprinkling faces
And cutting stays, as usual in such cases.

She said,—what could she say? Why, not a word:
   But the Count courteously invited in
The stranger, much appeased by what he heard:
   "Such things, perhaps, we'd best discuss within,"
Said he; "don't let us make ourselves absurd
   In public, by a scene, nor raise a din,
For then the chief and only satisfaction
Will be much quizzing on the whole transaction."

They entered, and for coffee called—it came,
   A beverage for Turks and Christians both,

Although the way they make it's not the same.
  Now Laura, much recovered, or less loth
To speak, cries "Beppo! what's your pagan name?
  Bless me! your beard is of amazing growth!
And how came you to keep away so long?
Are you not sensible 'twas very wrong?

"And are you *really, truly,* now a Turk?
  With any other women did you wive?
It's true they use their fingers for a fork?
  Well, that's the prettiest shawl—as I'm alive!
You'll give it me? They say you eat no pork.
  And how so many years did you contrive
To—bless me! did I ever? No, I never
Saw a man grown so yellow! How's your liver?

"Beppo! that beard of yours becomes you not;
  It shall be shaved before you're a day older:
Why do you wear it? Oh! I had forgot—
  Pray don't you think the weather here is colder?
How do I look? You shan't stir from this spot
  In that queer dress, for fear that some beholder
Should find you out, and make the story known.
How short your hair is! Lord! how grey it's grown!"

What answer Beppo made to these demands
  Is more than I know. He was cast away
About where Troy stood once, and nothing stands;
  Became a slave of course, and for his pay
Had bread and bastinadoes, till some bands
  Of pirates landing in a neighbouring bay,
He joined the rogues and prospered, and became
A renegado of indifferent fame.

But he grew rich, and with his riches grew so
    Keen the desire to see his home again,
He thought himself in duty bound to do so,
    And not be always thieving on the main;
Lonely he felt, at times, as Robin Crusoe,
    And so he hired a vessel come from Spain,
Bound for Corfu: she was a fine polacca,
Manned with twelve hands, and laden with tobacco.

Himself, and much (heaven knows how gotten!) cash,
    He then embarked, with risk of life and limb,
And got clear off, although the attempt was rash;
    He said that *Providence* protected him—
For my part, I say nothing—lest we clash
    In our opinions:—well, the ship was trim,
Set sail, and kept her reckoning fairly on,
Except three days of calm when off Cape Bonn.

They reached the island, he transferred his lading,
    And self and livestock to another bottom,
And passed for a true Turkey-merchant, trading
    With goods of various names, but I've forgot 'em.
However, he got off by this evading,
    Or else the people would perhaps have shot him;
And thus at Venice landed to reclaim
His wife, religion, house, and Christian name.

His wife received, the patriarch re-baptised him,
    (He made the church a present, by the way;)
He then threw off the garments which disguised him,
    And borrowed the Count's smallclothes for a day:
His friends the more for his long absence prized him,
    Finding he'd wherewithal to make them gay,

With dinners, where he oft became the laugh of them,
For stories—but *I* don't believe the half of them.

Whate'er his youth had suffered, his old age
   With wealth and talking made him some amends;
Though Laura sometimes put him in a rage,
   I've heard the Count and he were always friends.
My pen is at the bottom of a page,
   Which being finished, here the story ends;
'Tis to be wished it had been sooner done,
But stories somehow lengthen when begun.

The Vision of Judgement

Saint Peter sat by the celestial gate,
   His keys were rusty, and the lock was dull,
So little trouble had been given of late;
   Not that the place by any means was full,
But since the Gallic era "eighty-eight,"
   The devils had ta'en a longer, stronger pull,
And "a pull altogether," as they say
At sea—which drew most souls another way.

The angels all were singing out of tune,
   And hoarse with having little else to do,
Excepting to wind up the sun and moon,
   Or curb a runaway young star or two,
Or wild colt of a comet, which too soon
   Broke out of bounds o'er the ethereal blue,
Splitting some planet with its playful tail,
As boats are sometimes by a wanton whale.

The guardian seraphs had retired on high,
    Finding their charges past all care below;
Terrestrial business fill'd nought in the sky
    Save the recording angel's black bureau;
Who found, indeed, the facts to multiply
    With such rapidity of vice and woe,
That he had stripp'd off both his wings in quills,
And yet was in arrear of human ills.

His business so augmented of late years,
    That he was forced, against his will, no doubt,
(Just like those cherubs, earthly ministers)
    For some resource to turn himself about,
And claim the help of his celestial peers,
    To aid him ere he should be quite worn out
By the increased demand for his remarks;
Six angels and twelve saints were named his clerks.

This was a handsome board—at least for heaven;
    And yet they had even then enough to do,
So many conquerors' cars were daily driven,
    So many kingdoms fitted up anew;
Each day too slew its thousands six or seven,
    Till at the crowning carnage, Waterloo,
They threw their pens down in divine disgust—
The page was so besmear'd with blood and dust.

This by the way; 'tis not mine to record
    What angels shrink from: even the very devil
On this occasion his own work abhorr'd,
    So surfeited with the infernal revel;
Though he himself had sharpen'd every sword,
    It almost quench'd his innate thirst of evil.

(Here Satan's sole good work deserves insertion—
'Tis, that he has both generals in reversion.)

Let's skip a few short years of hollow peace,
   Which peopled earth no better, hell as wont,
And heaven none—they form the tyrant's lease
   With nothing but new names subscribed upon 't;
'Twill one day finish: meantime they increase,
   "With seven heads and ten horns," and all in front,
Like Saint John's foretold beast; but ours are born
Less formidable in the head than horn.

In the first year of freedom's second dawn
   Died George the Third; although no tyrant, one
Who shielded tyrants, till each sense withdrawn
   Left him nor mental nor external sun:
A better farmer ne'er brush'd dew from lawn,
   A weaker king never left a realm undone!
He died—but left his subjects still behind,
One half as mad—and t'other no less blind.

He died!—his death made no great stir on earth;
   His burial made some pomp; there was profusion
Of velvet, gilding, brass, and no great dearth
   Of aught but tears—save those shed by collusion;
For these things may be bought at their true worth:
   Of elegy there was the due infusion—
Bought also; and the torches, cloaks, and banners,
Heralds, and relics of old Gothic manners,

Form'd a sepulchral melo-drame. Of all
   The fools who flock'd to swell or see the show,
Who cared about the corpse? The funeral
   Made the attraction, and the black the woe.

There throbb'd not there a thought which pierced the pall;
 And when the gorgeous coffin was laid low,
It seem'd the mockery of hell to fold
The rottenness of eighty years in gold.

So mix his body with the dust! It might
 Return to what it *must* far sooner, were
The natural compound left alone to fight
 Its way back into earth, and fire, and air;
But the unnatural balsams merely blight
 What nature made him at his birth, as bare
As the mere million's base unmummied clay—
Yet all his spices but prolong decay.

He's dead—and upper earth with him has done:
 He's buried; save the undertaker's bill,
Or lapidary scrawl, the world is gone
 For him, unless he left a German will;
But where's the proctor who will ask his son?
 In whom his qualities are reigning still,
Except that household virtue, most uncommon,
Of constancy to an unhandsome woman.

"God save the king!" It is a large economy
 In God to save the like; but if he will
Be saving, all the better; for not one am I
 Of those who think damnation better still:
I hardly know too if not quite alone am I
 In this small hope of bettering future ill
By circumscribing, with some slight restriction,
The eternity of hell's hot jurisdiction.

I know this is unpopular; I know
 'Tis blasphemous; I know one may be damn'd

For hoping no one else may e'er be so;
   I know my catechism; I know we are cramm'd
With the best doctrines till we quite o'erflow;
   I know that all save England's church have shamm'd,
And that the other twice two hundred churches
And synagogues have made a *damn'd* bad purchase.

God help us all! God help me too! I am,
   God knows, as helpless as the devil can wish,
And not a whit more difficult to damn
   Than is to bring to land a late-hook'd fish,
Or to the butcher to purvey the lamb;
   Not that I'm fit for such a noble dish
As one day will be that immortal fry
Of almost every body born to die.

Saint Peter sat by the celestial gate,
   And nodded o'er his keys; when lo! there came
A wond'rous noise he had not heard of late—
   A rushing sound of wind, and stream, and flame;
In short, a roar of things extremely great,
   Which would have made aught save a saint exclaim;
But he, with first a start and then a wink,
Said, "There's another star gone out, I think!"

But ere he could return to his repose,
   A cherub flapp'd his right wing o'er his eyes—
At which Saint Peter yawn'd, and rubb'd his nose:
   "Saint porter," said the Angel, "prithee rise!"
Waving a goodly wing, which glow'd, as glows
   An earthly peacock's tail, with heavenly dyes;
To which the Saint replied, "Well, what's the matter?
Is Lucifer come back with all this clatter?"

"No," quoth the Cherub; "George the Third is dead."
  "And who *is* George the Third?" replied the Apostle;
"What George? what Third?" "The King of England," said
  The Angel. "Well! he won't find kings to jostle
Him on his way; but does he wear his head?
  Because the last we saw here had a tussle,
And ne'er would have got into heaven's good graces,
Had he not flung his head in all our faces.

"He was, if I remember, king of France;
  That head of his, which could not keep a crown
On earth, yet ventured in my face to advance
  A claim to those of martyrs—like my own:
If I had had my sword, as I had once
  When I cut ears off, I had cut him down;
But having but my *keys,* and not my brand,
I only knock'd his head from out his hand.

"And then he set up such a headless howl,
  That all the saints came out, and took him in;
And there he sits by St. Paul, cheek by jowl;
  That fellow Paul—the parvenu! The skin
Of Saint Bartholomew, which makes his cowl
  In heaven, and upon earth redeem'd his sin
So as to make a martyr, never sped
Better than did this weak and wooden head.

"But had it come up here upon its shoulders,
  There would have been a different tale to tell:
The fellow feeling in the saint's beholders
  Seems to have acted on them like a spell,
And so this very foolish head heaven solders
  Back on its trunk: it may be very well,

And seems the custom here to overthrow
Whatever has been wisely done below."

The Angel answer'd, "Peter! do not pout;
    The king who comes has head and all entire,
And never knew much what it was about—
    He did as doth the puppet—by its wire,
And will be judged like all the rest, no doubt:
    My business and your own is not to inquire
Into such matters, but to mind our cue—
Which is to act as we are bid to do."

While thus they spake, the angelic caravan,
    Arriving like a rush of mighty wind,
Cleaving the fields of space, as doth the swan
    Some silver stream (say Ganges, Nile, or Inde,
Or Thames, or Tweed) and midst them an old man
    With an old soul, and both extremely blind,
Halted before the gate, and in his shroud
Seated their fellow-traveller on a cloud.

But bringing up the rear of this bright host
    A Spirit of a different aspect waved
His wings, like thunder-clouds above some coast
    Whose barren beach with frequent wrecks is paved;
His brow was like the deep when tempest-tost;
    Fierce and unfathomable thoughts engraved
Eternal wrath on his immortal face,
And *where* he gazed a gloom pervaded space.

As he drew near, he gazed upon the gate
    Ne'er to be enter'd more by him or sin,
With such a glance of supernatural hate,
    As made Saint Peter wish himself within;

He potter'd with his keys at a great rate,
  And sweated through his apostolic skin:
Of course his perspiration was but ichor,
Or some such other spiritual liquor.

The very cherubs huddled altogether,
  Like birds when soars the falcon; and they felt
A tingling to the tip of every feather,
  And form'd a circle like Orion's belt
Around their poor old charge; who scarce knew whither
  His guards had led him, though they gently dealt
With royal manes (for by many stories,
And true, we learn the angels all are Tories).

As things were in this posture, the gate flew
  Asunder, and the flashing of its hinges
Flung over space an universal hue
  Of many-coloured flame, until its tinges
Reach'd even our speck of earth, and made a new
  Aurora borealis spread its fringes
O'er the North Pole; the same seen, when ice-bound,
By Captain Parry's crews, in "Melville's Sound."

And from the gate thrown open issued beaming
  A beautiful and mighty Thing of Light,
Radiant with glory, like a banner streaming
  Victorious from some world-o'erthrowing fight:
My poor comparisons must needs be teeming
  With earthly likenesses, for here the night
Of clay obscures our best conceptions, saving
Johanna Southcote, or Bob Southey raving.

'Twas the archangel Michael: all men know
  The make of angels and archangels, since

There's scarce a scribbler has not one to show,
   From the fiends' leader to the angels' prince.
There also are some altar-pieces, though
   I really can't say that they much evince
One's inner notions of immortal spirits;
But let the connoisseurs explain *their* merits.

Michael flew forth in glory and in good;
   A goodly work of him from whom all glory
And good arise; the portal past—he stood;
   Before him the young cherubs and saint hoary,
(I say *young,* begging to be understood
   By looks, not years; and should be very sorry
To state, they were not older than Saint Peter,
But merely that they seem'd a little sweeter).

The cherubs and the saints bow'd down before
   That arch-angelic Hierarch, the first
Of Essences angelical, who wore
   The aspect of a god; but this ne'er nurst
Pride in his heavenly bosom, in whose core
   No thought, save for his Maker's service, durst
Intrude, however glorified and high;
He knew him but the viceroy of the sky.

He and the sombre silent Spirit met—
   They knew each other both for good and ill;
Such was their power, that neither could forget
   His former friend and future foe; but still
There was a high, immortal, proud regret
   In either's eye, as if 'twere less their will
Than destiny to make the eternal years
Their date of war, and their "Champ Clos" the spheres.

But here they were in neutral space: we know
     From Job, that Satan hath the power to pay
A heavenly visit thrice a year or so;
     And that "the Sons of God," like those of clay,
Must keep him company; and we might show,
     From the same book, in how polite a way
The dialogue is held between the Powers
Of Good and Evil—but 'twould take up hours.

And this is not a theologic tract,
     To prove with Hebrew and with Arabic
If Job be allegory or a fact,
     But a true narrative; and thus I pick
From out the whole but such and such an act
     As sets aside the slightest thought of trick.
'Tis every tittle true, beyond suspicion,
And accurate as any other vision.

The spirits were in neutral space, before
     The gate of heaven; like eastern thresholds is
The place where Death's grand cause is argued o'er,
     And souls dispatched to that world or to this;
And therefore Michael and the other wore
     A civil aspect: though they did not kiss,
Yet still between his Darkness and his Brightness
There passed a mutual glance of great politeness.

The Archangel bowed, not like a modern beau,
     But with a graceful Oriental bend,
Pressing one radiant arm just where below
     The heart in good men is supposed to tend.
He turned as to an equal, not too low,
     But kindly; Satan met his ancient friend

With more hauteur, as might an old Castilian
Poor noble meet a mushroom rich civilian.

He merely bent his diabolic brow
    An instant; and then raising it, he stood
In act to assert his right or wrong, and show
    Cause why King George by no means could or should
Make out a case to be exempt from woe
    Eternal, more than other kings endued
With better sense and hearts, whom history mentions,
Who long have "paved hell with their good intentions."

Michael began: "What wouldst thou with this man,
    Now dead, and brought before the Lord? What ill
Hath he wrought since his mortal race began,
    That thou can'st claim him: Speak! and do thy will,
If it be just: if in this earthly span
    He hath been greatly failing to fulfil
His duties as a king and mortal, say,
And he is thine; if not, let him have way."

"Michael!" replied the Prince of Air, "even here,
    Before the gate of him thou servest, must
I claim my subject; and will make appear
    That as he was my worshipper in dust,
So shall he be in spirit, although dear
    To thee and thine, because nor wine nor lust
Were of his weaknesses; yet on the throne
He reign'd o'er millions to serve me alone.

"Look to *our* earth, or rather *mine; it* was,
    Once, more thy master's: but I triumph not
In this poor planet's conquest, nor, alas!
    Need he thou servest envy me my lot:

With all the myriads of bright worlds which pass
   In worship round him, he may have forgot
Yon weak creation of such paltry things;
I think few worth damnation save their kings,

"And these but as a kind of quit-rent, to
   Assert my right as lord; and even had
I such an inclination, 'twere (as you
   Well know) superfluous; they are grown so bad,
That hell has nothing better left to do
   Than leave them to themselves: so much more mad
And evil by their own internal curse,
Heaven cannot make them better, nor I worse.

"Look to the earth, I said, and say again:
   When this old, blind, mad, helpless, weak, poor worm,
Began in youth's first bloom and flush to reign,
   The world and he both wore a different form,
And much of earth and all the watery plain
   Of ocean call'd him king: through many a storm
His isles had floated on the abyss of Time;
For the rough virtues chose them for their clime.

"He came to his sceptre, young; he leaves it, old:
   Look to the state in which he found his realm,
And left it; and his annals too behold,
   How to a minion first he gave the helm;
How grew upon his heart a thirst for gold,
   The beggar's vice, which can but overwhelm
The meanest hearts; and for the rest, but glance
Thine eye along America and France!

" 'Tis true, he was a tool from first to last
   (I have the workmen safe); but as a tool

So let him be consumed! From out the past
    Of ages, since mankind have known the rule
Of monarchs—from the bloody rolls amass'd
    Of sin and slaughter—from the Caesar's school,
Take the worst pupil; and produce a reign
More drench'd with gore, more cumber'd with the slain!

"He ever warr'd with freedom and the free:
    Nations as men, home subjects, foreign foes,
So that they utter'd the word 'Liberty!'
    Found George the Third their first opponent. Whose
History was ever stain'd as his will be
    With national and individual woes?
I grant his household abstinence; I grant
His neutral virtues, which most monarchs want;

"I know he was a constant consort; own
    He was a decent sire, and middling lord.
All this is much, and most upon a throne;
    As temperance, if at Apicius' board,
Is more than at an anchorite's supper shown.
    I grant him all the kindest can accord;
And this was well for him, but not for those
Millions who found him what oppression chose.

"The new world shook him off; the old yet groans
    Beneath what he and his prepared, if not
Completed: he leaves heirs on many thrones
    To all his vices, without what begot
Compassion for him—his tame virtues; drones
    Who sleep, or despots who have now forgot
A lesson which shall be re-taught them, wake
Upon the throne of Earth; but let them quake!

"Five millions of the primitive, who hold
    The faith which makes ye great on earth, implored
A *part* of that vast *all* they held of old,—
    Freedom to worship—not alone your Lord,
Michael, but you, and you, Saint Peter! Cold
    Must be your souls, if you have not abhorr'd
The foe to Catholic participation
In all the licence of a Christian nation.

"True! he allow'd them to pray God; but as
    A consequence of prayer, refused the law
Which would have placed them upon the same base
    With those who did not hold the saints in awe."
But here Saint Peter started from his place,
    And cried, "You may the prisoner withdraw:
Ere Heaven shall ope her portals to this Guelf,
While I am guard, may I be damn'd myself!

"Sooner will I with Cerberus exchange
    My office (and *his* is no sinecure)
Than see this royal Bedlam bigot range
    The azure fields of heaven, of that be sure!"
"Saint!" replied Satan, "you do well to avenge
    The wrongs he made your satellites endure;
And if to this exchange you should be given,
I'll try to coax *our* Cerberus up to heaven."

Here Michael interposed: "Good saint! and devil!
    Pray not so fast; you both out-run discretion.
Saint Peter! you were wont to be more civil:
    Satan! excuse this warmth of his expression,
And condescension to the vulgar's level:
    Even saints sometimes forget themselves in session.

Have you got more to say?"—"No!"—"If you please,
I'll trouble you to call your witnesses."

Then Satan turn'd and wav'd his swarthy hand,
    Which stirr'd with its electric qualities
Clouds farther off than we can understand,
    Although we find him sometimes in our skies;
Infernal thunder shook both sea and land
    In all the planets, and hell's batteries
Let off the artillery, which Milton mentions
As one of Satan's most sublime inventions.

This was a signal unto such damn'd souls
    As have the privilege of their damnation
Extended far beyond the mere controls
    Of worlds past, present, or to come; no station
Is theirs particularly in the rolls
    Of hell assigned; but where their inclination
Or business carries them in search of game,
They may range freely—being damn'd the same.

They are proud of this—as very well they may,
    It being a sort of knighthood, or gilt key
Stuck in their loins; or like to an "entré"
    Up the back stairs, or such free-masonry:
I borrow my comparisons from clay,
    Being clay myself. Let not those spirits be
Offended with such base low likenesses;
We know their posts are nobler far than these.

When the great signal ran from heaven to hell,—
    About ten million times the distance reckon'd
From our sun to its earth, as we can tell
    How much time it takes up, even to a second,

For every ray that travels to dispel
   The fogs of London; through which, dimly beacon'd,
The weathercocks are gilt, some thrice a year,
   If that the *summer* is not too severe:—

I say that I can tell—'twas half a minute;
   I know the solar beams take up more time
Ere, pack'd up for their journey, they begin it;
   But then their telegraph is less sublime,
And if they ran a race, they would not win it
   'Gainst Satan's couriers bound for their own clime.
The sun takes up some years for every ray
To reach its goal—the devil not half a day.

Upon the verge of space, about the size
   Of half-a-crown, a little speck appear'd,
(I've seen a something like it in the skies
   In the Aegean, ere a squall); it near'd,
And, growing bigger, took another guise;
   Like an aerial ship it tack'd, and steer'd
Or *was* steer'd (I am doubtful of the grammar
Of the last phrase, which makes the stanza stammer;—

But take your choice); and then it grew a cloud,
   And so it was—a cloud of witnesses.
But such a cloud! No land ere saw a crowd
   Of locusts numerous as the heavens saw these;
They shadow'd with their myriads space; their loud
   And varied cries were like those of wild-geese,
(If nations may be liken'd to a goose)
And realized the phrase of "hell broke loose."

Here crash'd a sturdy oath of stout John Bull,
   Who damn'd away his eyes as heretofore:

There Paddy brogued "by Jasus!"—"What's your wull?"
   The temperate Scot exclaim'd: the French ghost swore
In certain terms I shan't translate in full,
   As the first coachman will; and midst the roar
The voice of Jonathan was heard to express,
"*Our* President is going to war, I guess."

Besides there were the Spaniard, Dutch, and Dane;
   In short, an universal shoal of shades
From Otaheite's Isle to Salisbury Plain,
   Of all climes and professions, years and trades,
Ready to swear against the good king's reign,
   Bitter as clubs in cards are against spades:
All summon'd by this grand "subpoena," to
Try if kings mayn't be damn'd, like me or you.

When Michael saw this host, he first grew pale,
   As angels can; next, like Italian twilight,
He turned all colours—as a peacock's tail,
   Or sunset streaming through a Gothic skylight
In some old abbey, or a trout not stale,
   Or distant lightning on the horizon *by* night,
Or a fresh rainbow, or a grand review
Of thirty regiments in red, green, and blue.

Then he address'd himself to Satan: "Why—
   My good old friend, for such I deem you, though
Our different parties make us fight so shy,
   I ne'er mistake you for a *personal* foe;
Our difference is *political,* and I
   Trust that, whatever may occur below,
You know my great respect for you; and this
Makes me regret whate'er you do amiss—

"Why, my dear Lucifer, would you abuse
    My call for witnesses? I did not mean
That you should half of earth and hell produce;
    'Tis even superfluous, since two honest, clean,
True testimonies are enough: we lose
    Our time, nay, our eternity, between
The accusation and defence: if we
Hear both, 'twill stretch our immortality."

Satan replied, "To me the matter is
    Indifferent, in a personal point of view:
I can have fifty better souls than this
    With far less trouble than we have gone through
Already; and I merely argued his
    Late Majesty of Britain's case with you
Upon a point of form: you may dispose
Of him; I've kings enough below, God knows!"

Thus spoke the Demon (late call'd "multifaced"
    By multo-scribbling Southey). "Then we'll call
One or two persons of the myriads placed
    Around our congress, and dispense with all
The rest," quoth Michael: "Who may be so graced
    As to speak first? there's choice enough—who shall
It be?" Then Satan answered, "There are many;
But you may choose Jack Wilkes as well as any."

A merry, cock-eyed, curious looking Sprite,
    Upon the instant started from the throng,
Drest in a fashion now forgotten quite;
    For all the fashions of the flesh stick long
By people in the next world; where unite
    All the costumes since Adam's, right or wrong,

From Eve's fig-leaf down to the petticoat,
Almost as scanty, of days less remote.

The Spirit look'd around upon the crowds
   Assembled, and exclaim'd, "My friends of all
The spheres, we shall catch cold amongst these clouds;
   So let's to business: why this general call?
If those are freeholders I see in shrouds,
   And 'tis for an election that they bawl,
Behold a candidate with unturn'd-coat!
Saint Peter, may I count upon your vote?"

"Sir," replied Michael, "you mistake: these things
   Are of a former life, and what we do
Above is more august; to judge of kings
   Is the tribunal met; so now you know."
"Then I presume those gentlemen with wings,"
   Said Wilkes, "are cherubs; and that soul below
Looks much like George the Third; but to my mind
A good deal older—Bless me! is he blind?"

"He is what you behold him, and his doom
   Depends upon his deeds," the Angel said.
"If you have ought to arraign in him, the tomb
   Gives licence to the humblest beggar's head
To lift itself against the loftiest."—"Some,"
   Said Wilkes, "don't wait to see them laid in lead,
For such a liberty—and I, for one,
Have told them what I thought beneath the sun."

"*Above* the sun repeat, then, what thou hast
   To urge against him," said the Archangel. "Why,"
Replied the Spirit, "since old scores are past,
   Must I turn evidence? In faith, not I.

Besides, I beat him hollow at the last,
    With all his Lords and Commons: in the sky
I don't like ripping up old stories, since
His conduct was but natural in a prince.

"Foolish, no doubt, and wicked, to oppress
    A poor unlucky devil without a shilling;
But then I blame the man himself much less
    Than Bute and Grafton, and shall be unwilling
To see him punish'd here for their excess,
    Since they were both damn'd long ago, and still in
Their place below; for me, I have forgiven,
And vote his 'habeas corpus' into heaven."

"Wilkes," said the Devil, "I understand all this;
    You turn'd to half a courtier ere you died,
And seem to think it would not be amiss
    To grow a whole one on the other side
Of Charon's ferry; you forget that *his*
    Reign is concluded; whatsoe'er betide,
He won't be sovereign more: you've lost your labour
For at the best he will but be your neighbour.

"However, I knew what to think of it,
    When I beheld you in your jesting way
Flitting and whispering round about the spit
    Where Belial, upon duty for the day,
With Fox's lard was basting William Pitt,
    His pupil; I knew what to think, I say:
That fellow even in hell breeds farther ills;
I'll have him *gagg'd*—'twas one of his own bills.

"Call Junius!" From the crowd a Shadow stalk'd,
    And at the name there was a general squeeze,

So that the very ghosts no longer walk'd
    In comfort, at their own aerial ease,
But were all ramm'd, and jamm'd (but to be balk'd,
    As we shall see) and jostled hands and knees,
Like wind compress'd and pent within a bladder,
Or like a human cholic, which is sadder.

The Shadow came! a tall, thin, gray-hair'd figure,
    That look'd as it had been a shade on earth;
Quick in its motions, with an air of vigour,
    But nought to mark its breeding or its birth:
Now it wax'd little, then again grew bigger,
    With now an air of gloom, or savage mirth;
But as you gazed upon its features, they
Changed every instant—to *what,* none could stay.

The more intently the ghosts gazed, the less
    Could they distinguish whose the features were;
The Devil himself seem'd puzzled even to guess;
    They varied like a dream—now here, now there;
And several people swore from out the press,
    They knew him perfectly; and one could swear
He was his father; upon which another
Was sure he was his mother's cousin's brother:

Another, that he was a duke, or knight,
    An orator, a lawyer, or a priest,
A nabob, a man-midwife; but the wight
    Mysterious changed his countenance at least
As oft as they their minds: though in full sight
    He stood, the puzzle only was increased;
The man was a phantasmagoria in
Himself—he was so volatile and thin!

The moment that you had pronounced him *one,*
   Presto! his face changed, and he was another;
And when that change was hardly well put on,
   It varied, till I don't think his own mother
(If that he had a mother) would her son
   Have known, he shifted so from one to t'other,
Till guessing from a pleasure grew a task,
At this epistolary "iron mask."

For sometimes he like Cerberus would seem—
   "Three gentlemen at once," (as sagely says
Good Mrs. Malaprop); then you might deem
   That he was not even *one;* now many rays
Were flashing round him; and now a thick steam
   Hid him from sight—like fogs on London days:
Now Burke, now Tooke, he grew to people's fancies,
And *certes* often like Sir Philip Francis.

I've an hypothesis—'tis quite my own;
   I never let it out till now, for fear
Of doing people harm about the throne,
   And injuring some minister or peer
On whom the stigma might perhaps be blown;
   It is—my gentle public, lend thine ear!
'Tis, that what Junius we are wont to call,
Was *really, truly,* nobody at all.

I don't see wherefore letters should not be
   Written without hands, since we daily view
Them written without heads; and books we see
   Are fill'd as well without the latter too:
And really till we fix on somebody
   For certain sure to claim them as his due,

Their author, like the Niger's mouth, will bother
The world to say if *there* be mouth or author.

"And who and what art thou?" the Archangel said.
   "For *that,* you may consult my title-page,"
Replied this mighty Shadow of a Shade:
   "If I have kept my secret half an age,
I scarce shall tell it now."—"Canst thou upbraid,"
   Continued Michael, "George Rex, or allege
Aught further?" Junius answer'd, "You had better
First ask him for *his* answer to my letter:

"My charges upon record will outlast
   The brass of both his epitaph and tomb."
"Repent'st thou not," said Michael, "of some past
   Exaggeration? something which may doom
Thyself, if false, as him if true? Thou wast
   Too bitter—is it not so? in thy gloom
Of passion?" "Passion!" cried the Phantom dim,
"I loved my country, and I hated him.

"What I have written, I have written: let
   The rest be on his head or mine!" So spoke
Old "Nominis Umbra"; and while speaking yet,
   Away he melted in celestial smoke.
Then Satan said to Michael, "Don't forget
   To call George Washington, and John Horne Tooke,
And Franklin":—but at this time there was heard
A cry for room, though not a phantom stirr'd.

At length with jostling, elbowing, and the aid
   Of cherubim appointed to that post,
The devil Asmodeus to the circle made
   His way, and look'd as if his journey cost

Some trouble. When his burden down he laid,
   "What's this?" cried Michael; "why, 'tis not a ghost?"
"I know it," quoth the incubus; "but he
Shall be one, if you leave the affair to me.

"Confound the Renegado! I have sprain'd
   My left wing, he's so heavy; one would think
Some of his works about his neck were chain'd.
   But to the point: while hovering o'er the brink
Of Skiddaw (where as usual it still rain'd),
   I saw a taper, far below me, wink,
And stooping, caught this fellow at a libel—
No less on History than the Holy Bible.

"The former is the devil's scripture, and
   The latter yours, good Michael; so the affair
Belongs to all of us, you understand.
   I snatch'd him up just as you see him there,
And brought him off for sentence out of hand:
   I've scarcely been ten minutes in the air—
At least a quarter it can hardly be:
I dare say that his wife is still at tea."

Here Satan said, "I know this man of old,
   And have expected him for some time here;
A sillier fellow you will scarce behold,
   Or more conceited in his petty sphere:
But surely it was not worth while to fold
   Such trash below your wing, Asmodeus dear!
We had the poor wretch safe (without being bored
With carriage) coming of his own accord.

"But since he's here, let's see what he has done."
   "Done!" cried Asmodeus, "he anticipates

The very business you are now upon,
    And scribbles as if head clerk to the Fates.
Who knows to what his ribaldry may run,
    When such an ass as this, like Balaam's, prates?"
"Let's hear," quoth Michael, "what he has to say;
You know we're bound to that in every way."

Now the Bard, glad to get an audience, which
    By no means often was his case below,
Began to cough, and hawk, and hem, and pitch
    His voice into that awful note of woe
To all unhappy hearers within reach
    Of poets when the tide of rhyme's in flow;
But stuck fast with his first hexameter,
Not one of all whose gouty feet would stir.

But ere the spavin'd dactyls could be spurr'd
    Into recitative, in great dismay
Both cherubim and seraphim were heard
    To murmur loudly through their long array;
And Michael rose ere he could get a word
    Of all his founder'd verses under way,
And cried, "For God's sake stop, my friend! 'twere best—
'Non Di, non homines—'you know the rest."

A general bustle spread throughout the throng,
    Which seem'd to hold all verse in detestation;
The angels had of course enough of song
    When upon service; and the generation
Of ghosts had heard too much in life, not long
    Before, to profit by a new occasion;
The Monarch, mute till then, exclaim'd, "What! what!
Pye come again? No more—no more of that!"

The tumult grew, an universal cough
  Convulsed the skies, as during a debate,
When Castlereagh has been up long enough,
  (Before he was first minister of state,
I mean—the *slaves hear now*); some cried "off, off,"
  As at a farce; till grown quite desperate,
The Bard Saint Peter pray'd to interpose
(Himself an author) only for his prose.

The varlet was not an ill-favour'd knave;
  A good deal like a vulture in the face,
With a hook nose and a hawk's eye, which gave
  A smart and sharper looking sort of grace
To his whole aspect, which, though rather grave,
  Was by no means so ugly as his case;
But that indeed was hopeless as can be,
Quite a poetic felony *"de se."*

Then Michael blew his trump, and still'd the noise
  With one still greater, as is yet the mode
On earth besides; except some grumbling voice,
  Which now and then will make a slight inroad
Upon decorous silence, few will twice
  Lift up their lungs when fairly overcrow'd;
And now the Bard could plead his own bad cause,
With all the attitudes of self-applause.

He said—(I only give the heads)—he said,
  He meant no harm in scribbling; 'twas his way
Upon all topics; 'twas, besides, his bread,
  Of which he butter'd both sides; 'twould delay
Too long the assembly (he was pleased to dread)
  And take up rather more time than a day,

To name his works—he would but cite a few—
Wat Tyler—Rhymes on Blenheim—Waterloo.

He had written praises of a regicide;
   He had written praises of all kings whatever;
He had written for republics far and wide,
   And then against them bitterer than ever;
For pantisocracy he once had cried
   Aloud, a scheme less moral than 'twas clever;
Then grew a hearty antijacobin—
Had turn'd his coat—and would have turn'd his skin.

He had sung against all battles, and again
   In their high praise and glory: he had call'd
Reviewing "the ungentle craft," and then
   Become as base a critic as ere crawl'd—
Fed, paid, and pamper'd by the very men
   By whom his muse and morals had been maul'd:
He had written much blank verse, and blanker prose,
And more of both than any body knows.

He had written Wesley's life:—here, turning round
   To Satan, "Sir, I'm ready to write yours,
In two octavo volumes, nicely bound,
   With notes and preface, all that most allures
The pious purchaser; and there's no ground
   For fear, for I can choose my own reviewers:
So let me have the proper documents,
That I may add you to my other saints."

Satan bow'd, and was silent. "Well, if you,
   With amiable modesty, decline
My offer, what says Michael? There are few
   Whose memoirs could be render'd more divine.

Mine is a pen of all work; not so new
    As it was once, but I would make you shine
Like your own trumpet; by the way, my own
Has more of brass in it, and is as well blown.

"But talking about trumpets, here's my Vision!
    Now you shall judge, all people; yes, you shall
Judge with my judgement! and by my decision
    Be guided who shall enter heaven or fall!
I settle all these things by intuition,
    Times present, past, to come, heaven, hell, and all,
Like King Alfonso! When I thus see double,
I save the Deity some worlds of trouble."

He ceased; and drew forth an MS; and no
    Persuasion on the part of devils, or saints,
Or angels, now could stop the torrent; so
    He read the first three lines of the contents;
But at the fourth, the whole spiritual show
    Had vanish'd, with variety of scents,
Ambrosial and sulphureous, as they sprang,
Like lightning, off from his "melodious twang."

Those grand heroics acted as a spell:
    The angels stopp'd their ears and plied their pinions;
The devils ran howling, deafen'd, down to hell;
    The ghosts fled, gibbering, for their own dominions—
(For 'tis not yet decided where they dwell,
    And I leave every man to his opinions);
Michael took refuge in his trump—but lo!
His teeth were set on edge, he could not blow!

Saint Peter, who has hitherto been known
    For an impetuous saint, upraised his keys,

And at the fifth line knock'd the Poet down;
    Who fell like Phaeton, but more at ease,
Into his lake, for there he did not drown,
    A different web being by the Destinies
Woven for the Laureate's final wreath, whene'er
Reform shall happen either here or there.

He first sunk to the bottom—like his works,
    But soon rose to the surface—like himself;
For all corrupted things are buoy'd, like corks,
    By their own rottenness, light as an elf,
Or wisp that flits o'er a morass: he lurks,
    It may be, still, like dull books on a shelf,
In his own den, to scrawl some "Life" or "Vision,"
As Wellborn says—"the devil turn'd precisian."

As for the rest, to come to the conclusion
    Of this true dream, the telescope is gone
Which kept my optics free from all delusion,
    And show'd me what I in my turn have shown:
All I saw farther in the last confusion,
    Was, that King George slipp'd into heaven for one;
And when the tumult dwindled to a calm,
I left him practising the hundredth psalm.

From *Don Juan*

DEDICATION

Bob Southey! You're a poet—poet Laureate,
    And representative of all the race;
Although 'tis true you turn'd out a Tory at
    Last,—yours has lately been a common case:—

And now, my epic renegade! what are ye at,
   With all the Lakers in and out of place?
A nest of tuneful persons, to my eye
Like four and twenty blackbirds in a pie;

"Which pie being open'd, they began to sing"—
   (This old song and new simile holds good)
"A dainty dish to set before the King,"
   Or Regent, who admires such kind of food.
And Coleridge, too, has lately taken wing,
   But, like a hawk encumber'd with his hood,
Explaining metaphysics to the nation—
I wish he would explain his Explanation.

You, Bob! are rather insolent, you know,
   At being disappointed in your wish
To supersede all warblers here below,
   And be the only Blackbird in the dish;
And then you overstrain yourself, or so,
   And tumble downward like the flying fish
Gasping on deck, because you soar too high, Bob,
And fall, for lack of moisture, quite adry, Bob!

And Wordsworth, in a rather long "Excursion,"
   (I think the quarto holds five hundred pages)
Has given a sample from the vasty version
   Of his new system to perplex the sages:
'Tis poetry—at least by his assertion,
   And may appear so when the dogstar rages;
And he who understands it would be able
To add a story to the Tower of Babel.

You, Gentlemen! by dint of long seclusion
   From better company have kept your own

At Keswick, and through still continued fusion
    Of one another's minds at last have grown
To deem as a most logical conclusion
    That Poesy has wreaths for you alone;
There is a narrowness in such a notion
Which makes me wish you'd change your lakes for ocean.

I would not imitate the petty thought,
    Nor coin my self-love to so base a vice,
For all the glory your conversion brought,
    Since gold alone should not have been its price.
You have your salary—was't for that you wrought?
    And Wordsworth has his place in the Excise.
You're shabby fellows—true—but poets still,
And duly seated on the immortal hill.

Your bays may hide the baldness of your brows,
    Perhaps some virtuous blushes—let them go,
To you I envy neither fruit nor boughs—
    And for the fame you would engross below
The field is universal, and allows
    Scope to all such as feel the inherent glow—
Scott, Rogers, Campbell, Moore, and Crabbe, will try
'Gainst you the question with posterity.

For me who, wandering with pedestrian Muses,
    Contend not with you on the winged steed,
I wish your fate may yield ye, when she chooses,
    The fame you envy, and the skill you need;
And recollect a poet nothing loses
    In giving to his brethren their full meed
Of merit, and complaint of present days
Is not the *certain* path to future praise.

He that reserves his laurels for posterity
   (Who does not often claim the bright reversion?)
Has generally no great crop to spare it, he
   Being only injured by his own assertion;
And although here and there some glorious rarity
   Arise, like Titan from the sea's immersion,
The major part of such appellants go
To—God knows where—for no one else can know.

If, fallen in evil days on evil tongues,
   Milton appeal'd to the Avenger, Time,
If Time, the Avenger, execrates his wrongs,
   And makes the word *"Miltonic"* mean *"sublime,"*
He deign'd not to belie his soul in songs,
   Nor turn his very talent to a crime—
He did not loathe the sire to laud the son,
But closed the tyrant-hater he begun.

Think'st thou, could he, the blind Old Man, arise
   Like Samuel from the grave, to freeze once more
The blood of monarchs with his prophecies,
   Or be alive again—again all hoar
With time and trials, and those helpless eyes
   And heartless daughters, worn, and pale, and poor,
Would *he* adore a sultan? *he* obey
The intellectual eunuch Castlereagh?

Cold-blooded, smooth-faced, placid miscreant!
   Dabbling its sleek young hands in Erin's gore,
And thus for wider carnage taught to pant,
   Transferr'd to gorge upon a sister-shore;
The vulgarest tool that tyranny could want,
   With just enough of talent, and no more,

To lengthen fetters by another fix'd,
And offer poison long already mix'd.

An orator of such set trash of phrase
    Ineffably, legitimately vile,
That even its grossest flatterers dare not praise,
    Nor foes—all nations—condescend to smile:
Not even a *sprightly* blunder's spark can blaze
    From that Ixion grindstone's ceaseless toil,
That turns and turns, to give the world a notion
Of endless torments, and perpetual motion.

A bungler even in its disgusting trade,
    And botching, patching, leaving still behind
Something of which its masters are afraid,
    States to be curb'd, and thoughts to be confined,
Conspiracy or Congress to be made—
    Cobbling at manacles for all mankind—
A tinkering slavemaker, who mends old chains,
With God and man's abhorrence for its gains.

If we may judge of matter by the mind,
    Emasculated to the marrow, *It*
Hath but two objects—how to serve, and bind,
    Deeming the chain it wears even men may fit;
Eutropius of its many masters—blind
    To worth as freedom, wisdom as to wit—
Fearless, because *no* feeling dwells in ice,
Its very courage stagnates to a vice.

Where shall I turn me not to *view* its bonds?
    For I will never *feel* them—Italy!
Thy late reviving Roman soul desponds
    Beneath the lie this state-thing breathed o'er thee;

Thy clanking chain, and Erin's yet green wounds,
    Have voices—tongues to cry aloud for me.
Europe has slaves, allies, kings, armies still,
And Southey lives to sing them very ill.

Meantime, Sir Laureate, I proceed to dedicate
    In honest, simple verse, this song to you;
And if in flattering strains I do not predicate,
    'Tis that I still retain my "buff and blue."
My politics, as yet, are all to educate,
    Apostasy's so fashionable too,
To keep *one* creed's a task grown quite Herculean,
Is it not so, my Tory ultra-Julian?

from CANTO 1

I want a hero: an uncommon want,
    When every year and month sends forth a new one,
Till, after cloying the gazettes with cant,
    The age discovers he is not the true one;
Of such as these I should not care to vaunt,
    I'll therefore take our ancient friend Don Juan,
We all have seen him in the pantomime
Sent to the devil, somewhat ere his time.

Vernon, the butcher Cumberland, Wolfe, Hawke,
    Prince Ferdinand, Granby, Burgoyne, Keppel, Howe,
Evil and good, have had their tithe of talk,
    And fill'd their sign-posts then, like Wellesley now;
Each in their turn like Banquo's monarchs stalk,
    Followers of fame, "nine farrow" of that sow:
France, too, had Buonaparté and Dumourier
Recorded in the Moniteur and Courier.

Barnave, Brissot, Condorcet, Mirabeau,
    Petion, Clootz, Danton, Marat, La Fayette,
Were French, and famous people, as we know;
    And there were others, scarce forgotten yet,
Joubert, Hoche, Marceau, Lannes, Dessaix, Moreau,
    With many of the military set,
Exceedingly remarkable at times,
But not at all adapted to my rhymes.

Nelson was once Britannia's god of war,
    And still should be so, but the tide is turn'd;
There's no more to be said of Trafalgar,
    'Tis with our hero quietly inurn'd;
Because the army's grown more popular,
    At which the naval people are concern'd;
Besides, the Prince is all for the land-service,
Forgetting Duncan, Nelson, Howe, and Jervis.

Brave men were living before Agamemnon
    And since, exceeding valorous and sage,
A good deal like him too, though quite the same none;
    But then they shone not on the poet's page,
And so have been forgotten:—I condemn none,
    But can't find any in the present age
Fit for my poem (that is, for my new one);
So, as I said, I'll take my friend Don Juan.

Most epic poets plunge in "medias res,"
    (Horace makes this the heroic turnpike road)
And then your hero tells, whene'er you please,
    What went before—by way of episode,
While seated after dinner at his ease,
    Beside his mistress in some soft abode,

Palace, or garden, paradise, or cavern,
Which serves the happy couple for a tavern.

That is the usual method, but not mine—
    My way is to begin with the beginning;
The regularity of my design
    Forbids all wandering as the worst of sinning,
And therefore I shall open with a line
    (Although it cost me half an hour in spinning)
Narrating somewhat of Don Juan's father,
And also of his mother, if you'd rather.

. . . .
The darkness of her oriental eye
    Accorded with her Moorish origin;
(Her blood was not all Spanish, by the by:
    In Spain, you know, this is a sort of sin).
When proud Grenada fell, and, forced to fly,
    Boabdil wept, of Donna Julia's kin
Some went to Africa, some staid in Spain,
Her great great grandmamma chose to remain.

She married (I forget the pedigree)
    With an Hidalgo, who transmitted down
His blood less noble than such blood should be;
    At such alliances his sires would frown,
In that point so precise in each degree
    That they bred *in and in,* as might be shown,
Marrying their cousins—nay, their aunts, and nieces,
Which always spoils the breed, if it increases.

This heathenish cross restored the breed again,
    Ruin'd its blood, but much improved its flesh;

For, from a root the ugliest in Old Spain
   Sprung up a branch as beautiful as fresh;
The sons no more were short, the daughters plain:
   But there's a rumour which I fain would hush,
'Tis said that Donna Julia's grandmamma
Produced her Don more heirs at love than law.

However this might be, the race went on
   Improving still through every generation,
Until it centr'd in an only son,
   Who left an only daughter; my narration
May have suggested that this single one
   Could be but Julia (whom on this occasion
I shall have much to speak about), and she
Was married, charming, chaste, and twenty-three.

Her eye (I'm very fond of handsome eyes)
   Was large and dark, suppressing half its fire
Until she spoke, then through its soft disguise
   Flash'd an expression more of pride than ire,
And love than either; and there would arise
   A something in them which was not desire,
But would have been, perhaps, but for the soul
Which struggled through and chasten'd down the whole.

Her glossy hair was cluster'd o'er a brow
   Bright with intelligence, and fair and smooth;
Her eyebrow's shape was like the aerial bow,
   Her cheek all purple with the beam of youth,
Mounting, at times, to a transparent glow,
   As if her veins ran lightning; she, in sooth,
Possess'd an air and grace by no means common:
Her stature tall—I hate a dumpy woman.

Wedded she was some years, and to a man
    Of fifty, and such husbands are in plenty;
And yet, I think, instead of such a ONE
    'Twere better to have TWO of five and twenty,
Especially in countries near the sun:
    And now I think on't, "mi vien in mente,"
Ladies even of the most uneasy virtue
Prefer a spouse whose age is short of thirty.

'Tis a sad thing, I cannot choose but say,
    And all the fault of that indecent sun,
Who cannot leave alone our helpless clay,
    But will keep baking, broiling, burning on,
That howsoever people fast and pray
    The flesh is frail, and so the soul undone:
What men call gallantry, and gods adultery,
Is much more common where the climate's sultry.
. . . .
Young Juan wander'd by the glassy brooks
    Thinking unutterable things; he threw
Himself at length within the leafy nooks
    Where the wild branch of the cork forest grew;
There poets find materials for their books,
    And every now and then we read them through,
So that their plan and prosody are eligible,
Unless, like Wordsworth, they prove unintelligible.

He, Juan, (and not Wordsworth) so pursued
    His self-communion with his own high soul,
Until his mighty heart, in its great mood,
    Had mitigated part, though not the whole
Of its disease; he did the best he could
    With things not very subject to control,

And turn'd, without perceiving his condition,
Like Coleridge, into a metaphysician.

He thought about himself, and the whole earth,
　　Of man the wonderful, and of the stars,
And how the deuce they ever could have birth;
　　And then he thought of earthquakes, and of wars,
How many miles the moon might have in girth,
　　Of air-balloons, and of the many bars
To perfect knowledge of the boundless skies;
And then he thought of Donna Julia's eyes.
. . . .
Here ends this canto.—Need I sing, or say,
　　How Juan, naked, favour'd by the night,
Who favours what she should not, found his way,
　　And reach'd his home in an unseemly plight?
The pleasant scandal which arose next day,
　　The nine days' wonder which was brought to light,
And how Alfonso sued for a divorce,
Were in the English newspapers, of course.

If you would like to see the whole proceedings,
　　The depositions, and the cause at full,
The names of all the witnesses, the pleadings
　　Of counsel to nonsuit, or to annul,
There's more than one edition, and the readings
　　Are various, but they none of them are dull,
The best is that in shorthand ta'en by Gurney,
Who to Madrid on purpose made a journey.

But Donna Inez, to divert the train
　　Of one of the most circulating scandals
That had for centuries been known in Spain,
　　Since Roderic's Goths, or older Genseric's Vandals,

First vow'd (and never had she vow'd in vain)
    To Virgin Mary several pounds of candles;
And then, by the advice of some old ladies,
She sent her son to be embark'd at Cadiz.

She had resolved that he should travel through
    All European climes, by land or sea,
To mend his former morals, or get new,
    Especially in France and Italy,
(At least this is the thing most people do).
    Julia was sent into a nunnery,
And there, perhaps, her feelings may be better
Shown in the following copy of her letter:

"They tell me 'tis decided; you depart:
    'Tis wise—'tis well, but not the less a pain;
I have no further claim on your young heart,
    Mine was the victim, and would be again;
To love too much has been the only art
    I used;—I write in haste, and if a stain
Be on this sheet, 'tis not what it appears,
My eyeballs burn and throb, but have no tears.

"I loved, I love you, for that love have lost
    State, station, heaven, mankind's, my own esteem,
And yet can not regret what it hath cost,
    So dear is still the memory of that dream;
Yet, if I name my guilt, 'tis not to boast,
    None can deem harshlier of me than I deem:
I trace this scrawl because I cannot rest—
I've nothing to reproach, nor to request.

"Man's love is of his life a thing apart,
    'Tis woman's whole existence; man may range

The court, camp, church, the vessel, and the mart,
   Sword, gown, gain, glory, offer in exchange
Pride, fame, ambition, to fill up his heart,
   And few there are whom these can not estrange;
Man has all these resources, we but one,
To love again, and be again undone."

. . . .

My poem's epic, and is meant to be
   Divided in twelve books; each book containing,
With love, and war, a heavy gale at sea,
   A list of ships, and captains, and kings reigning,
New characters; the episodes are three:
   A panorama view of hell's in training,
After the style of Virgil and of Homer,
So that my name of Epic's no misnomer.

All these things will be specified in time,
   With strict regard to Aristotle's rules,
The *vade mecum* of the true sublime,
   Which makes so many poets, and some fools;
Prose poets like blank-verse, I'm fond of rhyme,
   Good workmen never quarrel with their tools;
I've got new mythological machinery,
And very handsome supernatural scenery.

There's only one slight difference between
   Me and my epic brethren gone before,
And here the advantage is my own, I ween;
   (Not that I have not several merits more,
But this will more peculiarly be seen)
   They so embellish, that 'tis quite a bore
Their labyrinth of fables to thread through,
Whereas this story's actually true.

If any person doubt it, I appeal
   To history, tradition, and to facts,
To newspapers, whose truth all know and feel,
   To plays in five, and operas in three acts;
All these confirm my statement a good deal,
   But that which more completely faith exacts
Is, that myself, and several now in Seville,
Saw Juan's last elopement with the devil.

If ever I should condescend to prose,
   I'll write poetical commandments, which
Shall supersede beyond all doubt all those
   That went before; in these I shall enrich
My text with many things that no one knows,
   And carry precept to the highest pitch:
I'll call the work "Longinus o'er a Bottle,
Or, Every Poet his *own* Aristotle."

. . . .
But for the present, gentle reader! and
   Still gentler purchaser! the bard—that's I—
Must, with permission, shake you by the hand,
   And so your humble servant, and good bye!
We meet again, if we should understand
   Each other; and if not, I shall not try
Your patience further than by this short sample—
'Twere well if others follow'd my example.

"Go, little book, from this my solitude!
   I cast thee on the waters, go thy ways!
And if, as I believe, thy vein be good,
   The world will find thee after many days."
When Southey's read, and Wordsworth understood,
   I can't help putting in my claim to praise—

The four first rhymes are Southey's every line:
For God's sake, reader! take them not for mine.

from CANTO 2

At half-past eight o'clock, booms, hencoops, spars,
    And all things, for a chance, had been cast loose,
That still could keep afloat the struggling tars,
    For yet they strove, although of no great use:
There was no light in heaven but a few stars,
    The boats put off o'ercrowded with their crews;
She gave a heel, and then a lurch to port,
And, going down head foremost—sunk, in short.

Then rose from sea to sky the wild farewell,
    Then shriek'd the timid, and stood still the brave,
Then some leap'd overboard with dreadful yell,
    As eager to anticipate their grave;
And the sea yawn'd around her like a hell,
    And down she suck'd with her the whirling wave,
Like one who grapples with his enemy,
And strives to strangle him before he die.

And first one universal shriek there rush'd,
    Louder than the loud ocean, like a crash
Of echoing thunder; and then all was hush'd,
    Save the wild wind and the remorseless dash
Of billows; but at intervals there gush'd,
    Accompanied with a convulsive splash,
A solitary shriek, the bubbling cry
Of some strong swimmer in his agony.

The boats, as stated, had got off before,
    And in them crowded several of the crew;

And yet their present hope was hardly more
    Than what it had been, for so strong it blew
There was slight chance of reaching any shore;
    And then they were too many, though so few—
Nine in the cutter, thirty in the boat,
Were counted in them when they got afloat.

All the rest perish'd; near two hundred souls
    Had left their bodies; and, what's worse, alas!
When over Catholics the ocean rolls,
    They must wait several weeks before a mass
Takes off one peck of purgatorial coals,
    Because, till people know what's come to pass,
They won't lay out their money on the dead—
It costs three francs for every mass that's said.

Juan got into the long-boat, and there
    Contrived to help Pedrillo to a place;
It seem'd as if they had exchanged their care,
    For Juan wore the magisterial face
Which courage gives, while poor Pedrillo's pair
    Of eyes were crying for their owner's case:
Battista, though, (a name call'd shortly Tita)
Was lost by getting at some aqua-vita.

Pedro, his valet, too, he tried to save,
    But the same cause, conducive to his loss,
Left him so drunk, he jump'd into the wave
    As o'er the cutter's edge he tried to cross,
And so he found a wine-and-watery grave;
    They could not rescue him although so close,
Because the sea ran higher every minute,
And for the boat—the crew kept crowding in it.

A small old spaniel,—which had been Don Jóse's,
    His father's, whom he loved, as ye may think,
For on such things the memory reposes
    With tenderness,—stood howling on the brink,
Knowing, (dogs have such intellectual noses!)
    No doubt, the vessel was about to sink;
And Juan caught him up, and ere he stepp'd
Off, threw him in, then after him he leap'd.
. . . .
And thus it was with this our hapless crew,
    For on the third day there came on a calm,
And though at first their strength it might renew,
    And lying on their weariness like balm,
Lull'd them like turtles sleeping on the blue
    Of ocean, when they woke they felt a qualm,
And fell all ravenously on their provision,
Instead of hoarding it with due precision.

The consequence was easily foreseen—
    They ate up all they had, and drank their wine,
In spite of all remonstrances, and then
    On what, in fact, next day were they to dine?
They hoped the wind would rise, these foolish men!
    And carry them to shore; these hopes were fine,
But as they had but one oar, and that brittle,
It would have been more wise to save their victual.

The fourth day came, but not a breath of air,
    And Ocean slumber'd like an unwean'd child:
The fifth day, and their boat lay floating there,
    The sea and sky were blue, and clear, and mild—
With their one oar (I wish they had had a pair)
    What could they do? and hunger's rage grew wild:

So Juan's spaniel, spite of his entreating,
Was kill'd, and portion'd out for present eating.

On the sixth day they fed upon his hide,
   And Juan, who had still refused, because
The creature was his father's dog that died,
   Now feeling all the vulture in his jaws,
With some remorse received (though first denied)
   As a great favour one of the fore-paws,
Which he divided with Pedrillo, who
Devour'd it, longing for the other too.

The seventh day, and no wind—the burning sun
   Blister'd and scorch'd, and, stagnant on the sea,
They lay like carcases; and hope was none,
   Save in the breeze that came not; savagely
They glared upon each other—all was done,
   Water, and wine, and food,—and you might see
The longings of the cannibal arise
(Although they spoke not) in their wolfish eyes.

At length one whisper'd his companion, who
   Whisper'd another, and thus it went round,
And then into a hoarser murmur grew,
   An ominous, and wild, and desperate sound,
And when his comrade's thought each sufferer knew,
   'Twas but his own, suppress'd till now, he found:
And out they spoke of lots for flesh and blood,
And who should die to be his fellow's food.

But ere they came to this, they that day shared
   Some leathern caps, and what remain'd of shoes;
And then they look'd around them, and despair'd,

And none to be the sacrifice would choose;
At length the lots were torn up, and prepared,
    But of materials that much shock the Muse—
Having no paper, for the want of better,
They took by force from Juan Julia's letter.

The lots were made, and mark'd, and mix'd, and handed,
    In silent horror, and their distribution
Lull'd even the savage hunger which demanded,
    Like the Promethean vulture, this pollution;
None in particular had sought or plann'd it,
    'Twas nature gnaw'd them to this resolution,
By which none were permitted to be neuter—
And the lot fell on Juan's luckless tutor.

He but requested to be bled to death:
    The surgeon had his instruments, and bled
Pedrillo, and so gently ebb'd his breath,
    You hardly could perceive when he was dead.
He died as born, a Catholic in faith,
    Like most in the belief in which they're bred,
And first a little crucifix he kiss'd,
And then held out his jugular and wrist.

The surgeon, as there was no other fee,
    Had his first choice of morsels for his pains;
But being thirstiest at the moment, he
    Preferr'd a draught from the fast-flowing veins:
Part was divided, part thrown in the sea,
    And such things as the entrails and the brains
Regaled two sharks, who follow'd o'er the billow—
The sailors ate the rest of poor Pedrillo.

The sailors ate him, all save three or four,
    Who were not quite so fond of animal food;
To these were added Juan, who, before
    Refusing his own spaniel, hardly could
Feel now his appetite increased much more;
    'Twas not to be expected that he should,
Even in extremity of their disaster,
Dine with them on his pastor and his master.

. . . .

Of poor Pedrillo something still remain'd,
    But was used sparingly,—some were afraid,
And others still their appetites constrain'd,
    Or but at times a little supper made;
All except Juan, who throughout abstain'd,
    Chewing a piece of bamboo, and some lead:
At length they caught two boobies, and a noddy,
And then they left off eating the dead body.

And if Pedrillo's fate should shocking be,
    Remember Ugolino condescends
To eat the head of his arch-enemy
    The moment after he politely ends
His tale; if foes be food in hell, at sea
    'Tis surely fair to dine upon our friends,
When shipwreck's short allowance grows too scanty,
Without being much more horrible than Dante.

from CANTO 3

Haidée and Juan carpeted their feet
    On crimson satin, border'd with pale blue;
Their sofa occupied three parts complete
    Of the apartment—and appear'd quite new;
The velvet cushions—(for a throne more meet)—

Were scarlet, from whose glowing centre grew
A sun emboss'd in gold, whose rays of tissue,
Meridian-like, were seen all light to issue.
. . . .
And now they were diverted by their suite,
    Dwarfs, dancing girls, black eunuchs, and a poet,
Which made their new establishment complete;
    The last was of great fame, and liked to show it:
His verses rarely wanted their due feet—
    And for his theme—he seldom sung below it,
He being paid to satirize or flatter,
As the psalm says, "inditing a good matter."

He praised the present, and abused the past,
    Reversing the good custom of old days,
An eastern antijacobin at last
    He turn'd, preferring pudding to *no* praise—
For some few years his lot had been o'ercast
    By his seeming independent in his lays,
But now he sung the Sultan and the Pacha
With truth like Southey and with verse like Crashaw.
. . . .
In France, for instance, he would write a chanson;
    In England, a six canto quarto tale;
In Spain, he'd make a ballad or romance on
    The last war—much the same in Portugal;
In Germany, the Pegasus he'd prance on
    Would be old Goethe's—(see what says de Staël)
In Italy, he'd ape the "Trecentisti";
In Greece, he'd sing some sort of hymn like this t'ye:

        The isles of Greece, the isles of Greece!
            Where burning Sappho loved and sung,

Where grew the arts of war and peace,—
   Where Delos rose, and Phoebus sprung!
Eternal summer gilds them yet,
But all, except their sun, is set.

The Scian and the Teian muse,
   The hero's harp, the lover's lute,
Have found the fame your shores refuse;
   Their place of birth alone is mute
To sounds which echo further west
Than your sires' "Islands of the Blest."

The mountains look on Marathon—
   And Marathon looks on the sea;
And musing there an hour alone,
   I dream'd that Greece might still be free;
For standing on the Persian's grave,
I could not deem myself a slave.

A king sate on the rocky brow
   Which looks o'er sea-born Salamis;
And ships, by thousands, lay below,
   And men in nations;—all were his!
He counted them at break of day—
And when the sun set where were they?

And where are they? and where art thou,
   My country? On thy voiceless shore
The heroic lay is tuneless now—
   The heroic bosom beats no more!
And must thy lyre, so long divine,
Degenerate into hands like mine?

'Tis something, in the dearth of fame,
　　Though link'd among a fetter'd race,
To feel at least a patriot's shame,
　　Even as I sing, suffuse my face;
For what is left the poet here?
For Greeks a blush—for Greece a tear.

Must *we* but weep o'er days more blest?
　　Must *we* but blush?—Our fathers bled.
Earth! render back from out thy breast
　　A remnant of our Spartan dead!
Of the three hundred grant but three,
To make a new Thermopylae!

What, silent still? and silent all?
　　Ah! no;—the voices of the dead
Sound like a distant torrent's fall,
　　And answer, "Let one living head,
But one arise,—we come, we come!"
'Tis but the living who are dumb.

In vain—in vain: strike other chords;
　　Fill high the cup with Samian wine!
Leave battles to the Turkish hordes,
　　And shed the blood of Scio's vine!
Hark! rising to the ignoble call—
How answers each bold bacchanal!

You have the Pyrrhic dance as yet,
　　Where is the Pyrrhic phalanx gone?
Of two such lessons, why forget
　　The nobler and the manlier one?
You have the letters Cadmus gave—
Think ye he meant them for a slave?

Fill high the bowl with Samian wine!
   We will not think of themes like these!
It made Anacreon's song divine:
   He served—but served Polycrates—
A tyrant; but our masters then
Were still, at least, our countrymen.

The tyrant of the Chersonese
   Was freedom's best and bravest friend;
That tyrant was Miltiades!
   Oh! that the present hour would lend
Another despot of the kind!
Such chains as his were sure to bind.

Fill high the bowl with Samian wine!
   On Suli's rock, and Parga's shore,
Exists the remnant of a line
   Such as the Doric mothers bore;
And there, perhaps, some seed is sown,
The Heracleidan blood might own.

Trust not for freedom to the Franks—
   They have a king who buys and sells:
In native swords, and native ranks,
   The only hope of courage dwells;
But Turkish force, and Latin fraud,
Would break your shield, however broad.

Fill high the bowl with Samian wine!
   Our virgins dance beneath the shade—
I see their glorious black eyes shine;
   But gazing on each glowing maid,
My own the burning tear-drop laves,
To think such breasts must suckle slaves.

Place me on Sunium's marbled steep,
 Where nothing, save the waves and I,
May hear our mutual murmurs sweep;
 There, swan-like, let me sing and die:
A land of slaves shall ne'er be mine—
Dash down yon cup of Samian wine!

Thus sung, or would, or could, or should have sung,
 The modern Greek, in tolerable verse;
If not like Orpheus quite, when Greece was young,
 Yet in these times he might have done much worse:
His strain display'd some feeling—right or wrong;
 And feeling, in a poet, is the source
Of others' feeling; but they are such liars,
And take all colours—like the hands of dyers.

But words are things, and a small drop of ink,
 Falling like dew, upon a thought, produces
That which makes thousands, perhaps millions, think;
 'Tis strange, the shortest letter which man uses
Instead of speech, may form a lasting link
 Of ages; to what straits old Time reduces
Frail man, when paper—even a rag like this,
Survives himself, his tomb, and all that's his.

. . . .

Milton's the prince of poets—so we say;
 A little heavy, but no less divine:
An independent being in his day—
 Learn'd, pious, temperate in love and wine;
But his life falling into Johnson's way,
 We're told this great high priest of all the Nine
Was whipt at college—a harsh sire—odd spouse,
For the first Mrs Milton left his house.

All these are, *certes,* entertaining facts,
  Like Shakespeare's stealing deer, Lord Bacon's bribes;
Like Titus' youth, and Caesar's earliest acts;
  Like Burns (whom Doctor Currie well describes);
Like Cromwell's pranks;—but although truth exacts
  These amiable descriptions from the scribes,
As most essential to their hero's story,
They do not much contribute to his glory.

All are not moralists, like Southey, when
  He prated to the world of "Pantisocrasy";
Or Wordsworth unexcised, unhired, who then
  Season'd his pedlar poems with democracy;
Or Coleridge, long before his flighty pen
  Lent to the Morning Post its aristocracy;
When he and Southey, following the same path,
Espoused two partners (milliners of Bath.)
. . . .
But let me to my story: I must own,
  If I have any fault, it is digression;
Leaving my people to proceed alone,
  While I soliloquize beyond expression;
But these are my addresses from the throne,
  Which put off business to the ensuing session:
Forgetting each omission is a loss to
The world, not quite so great as Ariosto.

I know that what our neighbours call *"longueurs,"*
  (We've not so good a *word,* but have the *thing*
In that complete perfection which ensures
  An epic from Bob Southey every spring—)
Form not the true temptation which allures
  The reader; but 'twould not be hard to bring

Some fine examples of the *épopée*,
To prove it grand ingredient is *ennui*.

We learn from Horace, Homer sometimes sleeps;
    We feel without him: Wordsworth sometimes wakes,
To show with what complacency he creeps,
   With his dear *"Waggoners,"* around his lakes;
He wishes for "a boat" to sail the deeps—
    Of ocean?—No, of air; and then he makes
Another outcry for "a little boat,"
And drivels seas to set it well afloat.

. . . .

"Pedlars," and "boats," and "waggons"! Oh! ye shades
    Of Pope and Dryden, are we come to this?
That trash of such sort not alone evades
    Contempt, but from the bathos' vast abyss
Floats scumlike uppermost, and these Jack Cades
    Of sense and song above your graves may hiss—
The "little boatman" and his "Peter Bell"
Can sneer at him who drew "Achitophel"!

from CANTO 8

The town was taken—whether he might yield
    Himself or bastion, little mattered now;
His stubborn valour was no future shield.
    Ismail's no more! The crescent's silver bow
Sunk, and the crimson cross glared o'er the field,
    But red with no *redeeming* gore: the glow
Of burning streets, like moonlight on the water,
Was imaged back in blood, the sea of slaughter.

All that the mind would shrink from of excesses;
    All that the body perpetrates of bad;

All that we read, hear, dream, of man's distresses;
  All that the Devil would do if run stark mad;
All that defies the worst which pen expresses;
  All by which Hell is peopled, or as sad
As Hell—mere mortals who their power abuse,—
Was here (as heretofore and since) let loose.

If here and there some transient trait of pity
  Was shown, and some more noble heart broke through
Its bloody bond, and saved perhaps some pretty
  Child, or an aged, helpless man or two—
What's this in one annihilated city,
  Where thousand loves, and ties, and duties grew?
Cockneys of London! Muscadins of Paris!
Just ponder what a pious pastime war is:

Think how the joys of reading a Gazette
  Are purchased by all agonies and crimes:
Or if these do not move you, don't forget
  Such doom may be your own in after times.
Meantime the taxes, Castlereagh, and debt,
  Are hints as good as sermons, or as rhymes.
Read your own hearts and Ireland's present story,
Then feed her famine fat with Wellesley's glory.

But still there is unto a patriot nation,
  Which loves so well its country and its King,
A subject of sublimest exultation—
  Bear it, ye Muses, on your brightest wing!
Howe'er the mighty locust, Desolation,
  Strip your green fields, and to your harvests cling,
Gaunt Famine never shall approach the throne—
Though Ireland starve, great George weighs twenty stone.

from CANTO 16

A noise like to wet fingers drawn on glass,
　　Which sets the teeth on edge; and a slight clatter
Like showers which on the midnight gusts will pass,
　　Sounding like very supernatural water,
Came over Juan's ear, which throbbed, alas!
　　For immaterialism's a serious matter;
So that even those whose faith is the most great
In souls immortal, shun them *tête-à-tête.*

Were his eyes open?—Yes! and his mouth too.
　　Surprise has this effect—to make one dumb,
Yet leave the gate which Eloquence slips through
　　As wide as if a long speech were to come.
Nigh and more nigh the awful echoes drew,
　　Tremendous to a mortal tympanum:
His eyes were open, and (as was before
Stated) his mouth. What opened next?—the door.

It opened with a most infernal creak,
　　Like that of Hell. "Lasciate ogni speranza
Voi che entrate!" The hinge seemed to speak,
　　Dreadful as Dante's Rima, or this stanza;
Or—but all words upon such themes are weak;
　　A single shade's sufficient to entrance a
Hero—for what is substance to a Spirit?
Or how is't *matter* trembles to come near it?

The door flew wide, not swiftly—but, as fly
　　The sea-gulls, with a steady, sober flight—
And then swung back; nor close—but stood awry,
　　Half letting in long shadows on the light,
Which still in Juan's candlesticks burned high,

For he had two, both tolerably bright,
And in the door-way, darkening Darkness, stood
The sable Friar in his solemn hood.

Don Juan shook, as erst he had been shaken
    The night before; but being sick of shaking,
He first inclined to think he had been mistaken,
    And then to be ashamed of such mistaking;
His own internal ghost began to awaken
    Within him, and to quell his corporal quaking—
Hinting that soul and body on the whole
Were odds against a disembodied soul.

And then his dread grew wrath, and his wrath fierce;
    And he arose, advanced—the shade retreated;
But Juan, eager now the truth to pierce,
    Followed, his veins no longer cold, but heated,
Resolved to thrust the mystery carte and tierce,
    At whatsoever risk of being defeated:
The ghost stopped, menaced, then retired, until
He reached the ancient wall, then stood stone still.

Juan put forth one arm—Eternal Powers!
    It touched no soul, nor body, but the wall,
On which the moonbeams fell in silvery showers
    Chequered with all the tracery of the hall;
He shuddered, as no doubt the bravest cowers
    When he can't tell what 'tis that doth appal.
How odd, a single hobgoblin's non-entity
Should cause more fear than a whole host's identity!

But still the shade remained; the blue eyes glared,
    And rather variably for stony death;
Yet one thing rather good the grave had spared,

The ghost had a remarkably sweet breath.
A straggling curl showed he had been fair-haired;
  A red lip, with two rows of pearls beneath,
Gleamed forth, as through the casement's ivy shroud
The moon peeped, just escaped from a grey cloud.

And Juan, puzzled, but still curious, thrust
  His other arm forth—Wonder upon wonder!
It pressed upon a hard but glowing bust,
  Which beat as if there was a warm heart under.
He found, as people on most trials must,
  That he had made at first a silly blunder,
And that in his confusion he had caught
Only the wall, instead of what he sought.

The ghost, if ghost it were, seemed a sweet soul
  As ever lurked beneath a holy hood:
A dimpled chin, a neck of ivory, stole
  Forth into something much like flesh and blood;
Back fell the sable frock and dreary cowl,
  And they revealed—alas! that ere they should!
In full, voluptuous, but *not o'er* grown bulk,
The phantom of her frolic Grace—Fitz-Fulke!

🍂 ABOUT THE EDITOR 🍂

Paul Muldoon was born in Northern Ireland in 1951 and now lives in the United States. He is generally regarded as the leading Irish poet of his generation. His Selected Poems 1968–1986 *was published in 1987 by The Ecco Press.*